Reading Ladders

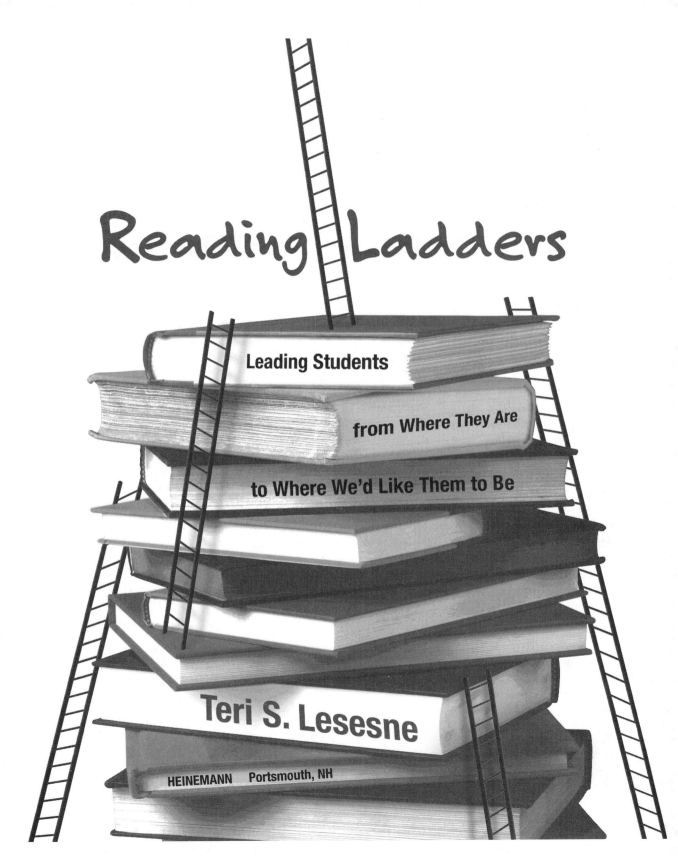

Reading Ladders

Leading Students

from Where They Are

to Where We'd Like Them to Be

Teri S. Lesesne

HEINEMANN   Portsmouth, NH

Heinemann

361 Hanover Street

Portsmouth, NH 03801–3912

www.heinemann.com

Offices and agents throughout the world

Library of Congress Cataloging-in-Publication Data

Lesesne, Teri S.

  Reading ladders : leading students from where they are to where we'd like them to be / Teri Lesesne.

    p. cm.

  Includes bibliographical references and index.

  ISBN 13: 978-0-325-01726-6

  ISBN 10: 0-325-01726-3

  1. Young adult literature, American—Study and teaching (Secondary). 2. Young adult literature—Study and teaching (Secondary). 3. Teenagers—Books and reading—United States. 4. Reading promotion. I. Title.

  PS490.L47 2009

  809'.892830712—dc22   2009033650

Editor: Lisa Luedeke

Production: Elizabeth Valway

Interior and cover design: Lisa Fowler

Composition: Achorn International

Manufacturing: Steve Bernier

Printed in the United States of America on acid-free paper

14 13 12 11 10 ML 1 2 3 4 5

Contents

Foreword

Gary Paulsen once described Dr. Teri Lesesne as "passionate . . . fierce and funny" when it came to her relationship with kids and books (Paulsen 2008, 73). Paulsen penned those words of tribute in an article coauthored with fellow YA authors Joan Bauer and Chris Crutcher for *The ALAN Review*. Teri had just won the 2007 ALAN Award for lifetime accomplishment in the field of young adult literature, and authors were lining up to pay their respects in print.

Teri (aka the Goddess of YA Literature) has truly invested a lifetime in making the world a better place through reading by finding the right books for young readers; in fact, her popular 2003 book is actually entitled *Making the Match: The Right Book for the Right Reader at the Right Time*.

However, once that match is made, and that young reader is hooked, and the last page of that first book has been turned—where do we go from there? In *Reading Ladders: Moving Students from Where They Are to Where We'd Like Them to Be*, Teri not only provides a plan for finding the next book, but the book after that, and the book after that, and many books after that. She appropriately names this series of books "reading ladders," which is the perfect analogy for helping students to climb up to more sophisticated and challenging texts one step, and one book, at a time.

The analogy of a ladder is perfect for describing what is most often lacking in our school curriculum: transitional literature. The first rung on a reading ladder is a book a reader already treasures, the ladder then moves up a rung at a time to more and more sophisticated literature, rising just fast enough to challenge the reader, but not so fast that it harms his or her love of reading.

Counterintuitively, but traditionally, we have expected our students to make the leap from chapter books to the oldest and most revered tomes in western civilization "with nary a bridge to help readers cross successfully," as Teri puts it, a practice which she calls "vertical reading" (Chapter 5, page 43).

I am frustrated, for example, when eighth-grade honor classes are assigned to read *The Lord of the Flies*, a book meant to illustrate the dark side of human nature through the most shocking and unlikely medium of male British private school students. The author, William Golding, intended this story as an allegory for the horrors of World War II as he experienced them as an adult. Interpreting the text well is an appropriate expectation for college readers, but Golding never meant it as literature for fourteen-year-old kids.

We need to ask ourselves: what did these eighth-grade students tackling *Lord of the Flies* read the year before in the seventh grade? *Harry Potter*? It's a pretty steep climb from there up to Golding's book. This is not to say that, using Teri's concept of reading ladders that a reader couldn't start with *Harry Potter* and one day climb to *Lord of the Flies,* but it should be a process that takes place over years, as the reader's skills of literary interpretation and emotional maturity grow. Vertical reading without the benefit of a "ladder" kills the love of reading. Keeping students in their Zone of Proximal Development (Vygotsky) through reading ladders nurtures it.

Reading ladders, as Teri envisions them, scaffold readers up through a variety of connectors: books written all by the same author, books written by similar authors, books from a single genre that grow more difficult, and so on. A Gary Paulsen reading ladder, for example, might begin with *Hatchet*, move through all four sequels about Brian Robeson, then go on to *Guts: The True Stories behind Hatchet and the Brian Books*, then on to *Dogsong*, followed by *Winter Dance: The Fine Madness of Running the Iditarod*, and so on. An outdoor adventure ladder might include books by Paulsen, as well as Will Hobbs and Ben Michaelsen, always keeping a lock on the young reader's interest while providing an increasing depth of plot, characterization and theme. Teri gives lots of guidance and step-by-step instructions on how to build ladders for young readers with various interests.

"But," your district curriculum director may say, "can these reading ladders help improve skills of literary interpretation?" (This is code for "raise our test scores"). The answer is yes; in fact, Teri's final chapter delves into some pretty impressive curriculum planning in which the reading ladders' rungs are based upon literary devices and their use, including hyperbole, metaphor and simile, personification, idiomatic language, and more. Some great poetry collections are included, but then no genre or format has been left out—from manga, to picture books, to graphic novels (more correctly referred to as sequential art narrative), to audio books. The readers benefit from Dr. Lesesne's extensive (scary!) knowledge of everything under the sun that kids might want to read (or listen to). And when kids read extensively, reading scores go up.

God bless Teri Lesesne for providing a logical, common sense, research-based explanation for using young adult literature, if not in place of, at least in conjunction with the classics. Through her new "Four Rs—rigor, relevance, relationships, and response" (3)—Teri dispels the myth that all young adult literature is lightweight fluff with hot pink covers or apprentice sorcerers on the front.

First, Teri supplies titles of books which are not just literarily substantial compared to other YA titles, but stand up quite nicely when compared to books written for any age reader, during any literary period over the centuries, such as Marcus Zusack's *The Book Thief*, or Robert Cormier's *The Chocolate War*. She also provides instructional approaches that demonstrate how to use engaging YA literature as a bridge into more difficult canonical selections, raising the probability of success for the latter (and ladder). *Beowulf* and *Macbeth* are even suggested later in the book.

So there we have *rigor*, but her case for *relevance* is even stronger. A book that has characters, locations, and situations (i.e., conflicts) that the readers may struggle with in their own daily lives can facilitate a connection so strong that they read straight through the night and write a letter to the author the next day asking how the writer knew so much about their life, and explaining how much it helped to see the situation through someone else's eyes for a change. Again, Lesesne gives examples of books, such as Laurie Halse Anderson's *Wintergirls*, and Chris Lynch's *Sins of the Father* that frequently touch such a chord with adolescents. These are books that feel almost autobiographical to some young people as they read them, and as Chris Crutcher once said, "Stories can help teenagers look at their feelings or come to emotional resolution…'I am not alone' is powerful medicine" (39).

The third and fourth Rs, *relationship* and *response*, are as much about the reader as they are about the book. Young adult literature provides opportunities for readers to develop relationships with books and to respond to books in ways that are often impossible when they read canonical literature.

As I travel around the nation, I always ask teens I encounter, "What are you reading? Who's your favorite author?" I cannot remember any young person whose face did not light up as she said, "*Twilight*," or "Stephenie Meyer," or as he said "Anything by Sherman Alexie," or "*Hunger Games*."

Unfortunately, as they read the traditional literary canon and write "responses" for school that are usually essays or "constructed responses" for tests, that light in their eyes fades and often disappears. These writings are not truly responses to the books but are, rather, the parroting of ideas. And are not the students' ideas, but the ideas of a heritage of literary critics who have passed judgment on the book over the years. This variety of writing fails to qualify as what writing pedagogy guru George Hillocks has called "real writing," writing of high cognitive function, which includes "inquiry, discovery, and meaning making" (10). On the other hand, hundreds of good YA books are coming out every year, books that can build strong relationships with readers and elicit intelligent, deeply thought out responses from those readers. Why not use them?

Early in this book, Teri points out that we develop the habits of lifelong readers over time. She explains how this happens: access to books, time to read, and reading modeled by older readers (including being read to out loud). I have fond memories of elementary school teachers reading entire books to me and my classmates, fifteen or twenty minutes a day, over the course of a few weeks. Some were fantasies, and some were historical fiction, such as *Ben and Me*, the story of how Benjamin Franklin was befriended by a mouse named Amos, who helped in the discovery of many things for which Franklin got sole credit. Forty-eight years later, I still remember most of that story, read to me at Wright Elementary School in Cedar Rapids, Iowa, when I was eight years old.

The world needs Teri Lesesne right now. Reading is in harm's way and needs a heroine. *Reading at Risk* (2004) a publication from the National Endowment for the Arts, reveals the results of surveys conducted by the U.S. Census Bureau measuring trends in reading from 1982–2002. These surveys indicate a frightening decline in literary reading among all adults, ages 18 and up, but with the largest drop, 28%, coming among 18–24 year olds (the surveys did not track people under 18) (xi).

Reading Ladders provides great hope, however, that we can lead young readers into the light, "*From Where They Are to Where We'd Like Them to Be*," just as the subtitle says. Teri's books, her blog, and website *www.professornana.com*, her conference presentations, her ceaseless mentoring of kids, teachers, and aspiring professors, and her relentless advocacy for young adult authors make a huge difference in the world. Many thanks to Teri for, as Joan Bauer puts it, ". . . matching books with readers and people with ideas that will change their lives" (Bauer 2008, 75)—once again.

—Jim Blasingame

Works Cited

Crutcher, Chris. 1992. "Healing Through Literature." *Authors' Insights: Turning Teenagers into Readers and Writers*, edited by Don Gallo, 33–40. Portsmouth, NH: Boynton/Cook.

Hillocks, George. 1995. *Teaching as Reflective Practice*. New York: Teachers College Press.

National Endowment for the Arts. 2004. *Reading At Risk: A Survey of Literary Reading in America Research Division Report #46.* http://www.nea.gov/pub/ReadingAtRisk.pdf (accessed September 15, 2009)

Paulsen, Gary, Joan Bauer, and Chris Crutcher. 2008. "A True Calling That Grows More Lovely Each Year." *The ALAN Review* (36)1 (Fall): 73.

Acknowledgments

One of my favorite movies is *All That Jazz*. There is a number about halfway through the movie called "Everything Old Is New Again." There is a great deal of truth in this title, but I would perhaps rephrase a bit less lyrically and say this: What we see touted as new actually has its roots in tradition, in history, in our past. The past plays an essential role in all of our lives. The person I am today is the result of tradition, of history, of the past. My own history includes some incredible people who provided me with the tools I needed to write this book.

Thanks to Dr. Richard F. Abrahamson, who took a handful of doctoral students and sent us off into the stacks to read back issues of *English Journal, The Journal of Reading,* and many other periodicals. What we discovered there was pure gold: the ideas and writings of Rosenblatt, Probst, Ley, Carlsen, and others. That was where I first learned about the concept of reading ladders. Reading the history of the field bit by bit in the journals of our profession was invaluable. If not for Dick and that class, so much of the tradition, the history, the past would be unknown and perhaps forgotten. Thanks, Dick, for continuing to be a mentor and friend who encourages me to write about how to connect kids to books.

Thanks go also to Kylene Beers, who insisted I had more to say and encouraged me to write this book. Who knew back when we were those green teachers that we would one day sit over lunch and talk about books we were writing?

Lois Buckman, my colleague and coconspirator on so many occasions, once again provided invaluable help in preparing the bibliography of trade books in Appendix A. She connects kids to books daily, and I admire her for all she continues to do for students in her role as librarian. Thanks, Lois, for being an inspiration to those students, to their teachers, and to me, too.

Thanks to the folks at Heinemann, who welcomed me as a new author and gave me tons of room and time to tell my story. Lisa Luedeke and Carol Schanche sent me comments that made me truly reenvision this book. I thank them for their careful, critical eyes.

Thanks to my colleagues in YA literature whose scholarship I use to inform my writing. ALAN and YALSA workshops allow me to network and to share in the experiences and stories of leaders in the field. I am incredibly fortunate to have found a home in both the teacher and librarian camps.

Thanks, especially, to my family for supporting me in my endeavors. It is not easy to live with someone who needs to be solitary from time to time. Thanks to Scout for letting me know, none too subtly, when it was time to take a break and play with him.

Finally, and long overdue, thanks to Henry, my husband and my companion on this and so many other life journeys. He listened patiently to complaints, ideas that were not fully formed, and the babblings of someone who talks to herself when she writes (or so he tells me). Not only is Henry my better half; he is what makes me whole when I feel less. None of this would be possible without you.

In the spirit of the book, here is a ladder of acknowledgments:

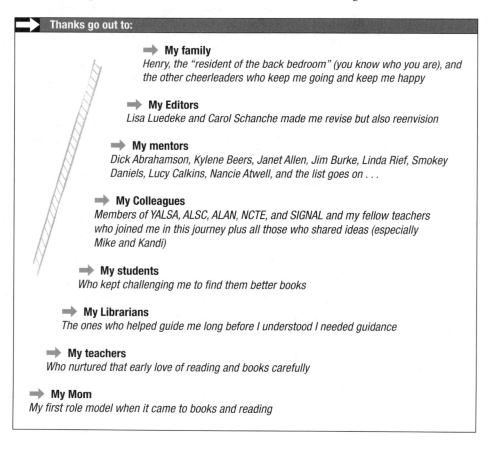

Thanks go out to:

My family
Henry, the "resident of the back bedroom" (you know who you are), and the other cheerleaders who keep me going and keep me happy

My Editors
Lisa Luedeke and Carol Schanche made me revise but also reenvision

My mentors
Dick Abrahamson, Kylene Beers, Janet Allen, Jim Burke, Linda Rief, Smokey Daniels, Lucy Calkins, Nancie Atwell, and the list goes on . . .

My Colleagues
Members of YALSA, ALSC, ALAN, NCTE, and SIGNAL and my fellow teachers who joined me in this journey plus all those who shared ideas (especially Mike and Kandi)

My students
Who kept challenging me to find them better books

My Librarians
The ones who helped guide me long before I understood I needed guidance

My teachers
Who nurtured that early love of reading and books carefully

My Mom
My first role model when it came to books and reading

Meeting Students Where They Are

WHY USE YA LITERATURE IN THE FIRST PLACE?

chapter

1

Recently, the person who was applying color to my gray hair tried to strike up a conversation by asking what I do for a living. When I replied that I taught children's and young adult literature to teachers and librarians, this young woman paused thoughtfully and asked me, "You mean you have to go to school to do that?" My initial reaction in such circumstances is to be indignant. However, when I pause to look at this innocent question from a different perspective, I know it is a legitimate question, one I need to answer in order to show those outside of education what we do and how tough our job can be. And those of us who work in the field of juvenile literature are often asked about how simple it must be to use "easy" books with our students. We need to be able to communicate to the naysayers in our communities and even in our schools that literature for teens is not some sort of dumbed-down version of real literature.

Recent articles in the field have talked about the need for literature to be *rigorous*. Of course, this term is often code for the work of classic authors who have been a part of the literary canon for decades. The works of Hawthorne and Hemingway, of

Faulkner and Fitzgerald, of Cooper and Dickens possess sufficient rigor to make them worthwhile for study in the English classroom. YA literature, some purists argue, does not possess the rigor of the classics. Therefore, it is deemed acceptable for recreational reading but not for classroom study. Indeed, the research does indicate that YA literature has made little if any progress in terms of being studied in the English curriculum, especially past middle school. Applebee's 1991 study examined the most frequently studied anthologies used in English classrooms and concluded that 86 percent of the selections were written by white authors, fewer than 25 percent of the authors were female, and almost 70 percent of the authors were from North America. The only contemporary (i.e., twenty-first-century) author was Maya Angelou, with excerpts from *I Know Why the Caged Bird Sings*. Shawn Bird, who replicated Applebee's work in 2005, found similar results. Literature anthologies, by and large, contained few selections from twenty-first-century books. This finding suggests another characteristic that is largely missing from the canon: relevance.

How relevant are the authors whose works are included in the literature anthologies used in so many classrooms? Poems such as "The Highwayman" and "Snowbound" and "Red Wheelbarrow" are often not relevant to today's readers. Longer works by Dickens and Twain and Cooper may also be out of reach in terms of their contemporary relevance. It is important to note that these authors were once contemporary authors writing about the trials and tribulations of their time. Sometimes those trials and tribulations do not transfer readily to students who are plugged in, online, and texting. How important is relevance and how can we connect students to contemporary books and eventually to the classics? These are questions I address in this book as I introduce the concept of reading ladders. Reading ladders can, among other things, help us take students from one level of reading to the next logical level.

I have mentioned two essential characteristics of literature thus far: rigor and relevance. To this short list I would add two other characteristics: relationships and response. Relationships and response are rather intertwined. Students often develop a relationship with an author or a genre. I recall Peter, who read the works of S. E. Hinton over and over again. He simply felt that this author "understood guys." The popularity of the vampire series by Stephenie Meyer is certainly proof of this relationship building. Tweens and teens stood in line for subsequent volumes in the Twilight series—*New Moon* (2006), *Eclipse* (2008b), and *Breaking Dawn* (2008a). New series such as The 39 Clues and The Hunger Games are also creating legions of fans who eagerly anticipate the next book. Sometimes the relationship is not about one author but a particular genre. One look at the American Library Association's "Best Books for Young Adults" lists from the past several years reveals a plethora of dystopic, futuristic novels. Vampire books abound, riding the coattails of the Meyer books, certainly. Look at the *New York Times* best-seller lists from week to week and notice the trends and fads that emerge.

Response is closely related to this forming of relationships. It may, in fact, be the reason why we form a close bond with an author, a series, or a genre or format. Somehow, this author or book or form or group of characters in a series strikes a resonant chord in us as readers. There have been so many books that have struck that chord for me. *Rosemary's Baby* scared the spit out of me and showed me that books could indeed make me shiver and even put my hands up in front of my face to somehow protect me from the evil emanating from the story. On the other hand, *Charles and Emma* (Heiligman 2009), *Hitler Youth* (Bartoletti 2005), and *King of the Mild Frontier* (Crutcher 2003) demonstrated that nonfiction could be as moving as fiction. Some books make readers question the motivation and actions of the characters, another form of response. Most readers of *Twilight* (Meyer 2005) and its sequels have remarked to me that, if they were Bella, they would have forced Edward's hand sooner.

Response also includes talking about the relative merits of the books we read. Is this a good book or a great book? What is the distinction between the two? After serving on several committees charged with selecting the most distinguished contribution to literature, this response has become almost second nature for me as a reader. We can develop this in our students as well by providing reading experiences that promote evaluative and critical responses.

Back in the "good" old days, we referred to the three Rs as reading, writing, and arithmetic. Today, I am proposing that we focus on the Four Rs: rigor, relevance, relationships, and response. Not only can young adult literature promote each and every one of these Rs, but reading ladders can help us help kids continue to grow and move forward as readers—and ultimately become independent. If students like certain types of books, certain genres, or certain qualities in a book, we can help them stretch by showing them books that mirror what they already like but that perhaps are *a little longer, a bit more abstract, or challenge them more.*

Perhaps some brief examples are in order before we progress further. You will note that I begin Chapter 2 with a metaphor about Lincoln Logs because of their simple and enduring nature. This book, like the long-beloved building toys and reading itself, begins with the basics, moves to the reimagined, and continues on to the ingenious. So, let's take a look at the basics right now: the Four Rs.

> Back in the "good" old days, we referred to the three Rs as reading, writing, and arithmetic. Today, I am proposing that we focus on the Four Rs: rigor, relevance, relationships, and response.

The Rigors of YA Literature

From its earliest incarnations, YA literature has suffered from a misconception that it is somehow less literary than *real* literature. Junior novel, teen lit, adolescent book: even these early terms for the literature carry negative connotations. I am willing to bet that you have encountered this apparent prejudice against using contemporary literature in the classroom, particularly for classroom study. I think those folks who would denigrate using YA literature fail to see that it has structure, style, and substance. It *is* worthy of scrutiny in the classroom. Let's begin with a handful of examples that illustrate the incredible depth of YA literature. These are the first of many examples that demonstrate the rigor present in contemporary books.

THE CHOCOLATE WAR BY ROBERT CORMIER

One of the earliest novels in the field of YA literature is still one of the touchstone books in the genre. Cormier's mastery of language and his incredible sense of style present readers with a novel that is Hemingway-esque in its sentence structure. Moreover, *The Chocolate War* (2004) offers wonderful examples of figurative language: symbolism, metaphor, simile, and the like. Jerry Renault, a student at Trinity High School, decides not to participate in the annual chocolate sale for the school. At first he does not sell the candy at the direction of Archie, the leader of a group called the Vigils at the school. Ultimately, though, Jerry defies Archie and the Vigils and even Brother Leon, the head of the school. When he takes this stance, Jerry puts himself squarely opposite those in power. He dares to disturb the universe and, in doing so, places his own life at risk. Cormier explores the themes of power that corrupts and peer pressure that causes individuals to go along with the crowd. Moreover, in novel after novel, Cormier deftly creates characters that readers will come to despise; he creates plots that are as far from predictable as can be; and he creates literature worthy of exploration in middle and high school classrooms.

SECOND SIGHT BY GARY BLACKWOOD

My husband reads a series of books by an adult author named Harry Turtledove. Turtledove's books take a historic event and turn it upside down, posing questions such as: What would have happened if Hitler had won World War II? My response to these books is less than enthusiastic. "But he *didn't*," I protest. However, it is this exploration of *what if* that is at the heart of all literature. So, when I read *Second Sight*, by Gary Blackwood (2005), I came to understand my husband's interest in this type of story. Blackwood presents two children who claim to be able to see into the future. One is doing so as part of a vaudeville act; the other truly possesses powers of ESP. She sees something terrible happening to President Lincoln at the theatre. How can two children get to the president and warn him of the danger? Further, how will their warning, once heeded, change the course of history? I would argue that in addition to mirroring some of the types of stories in adult literature, books such as this one also offer more questions than answers to readers. That is one of the hallmarks of a great story.

THE BOOK THIEF BY MARKUS ZUSAK

Winner of a Printz Honor Medal (the Printz Award is given each year for distinguished contribution to literature for young adults by the Young Adult Library Services Association of the American Library Association; think of this as the Newbery equivalent for young adult literature), *The Book Thief* (Zusak 2007) is set in Germany during World War II. That suggests yet another Holocaust novel, and surely we already have enough novels set in this time period. However, there is more to this story than the time period in which it is set. Part of what makes this book extraordinary is that the narrator is not the protagonist. The narrator is Death. This harrowing voice is at turns serious, ironic, sarcastic, and even humorous. Death observes our protagonist, a young girl named Leisel who is the book thief referred to in the novel's title. For Leisel, remaining alive and sane during the crazy times of Nazism requires relying on the power of books and reading. This novel pushes the envelope in what we have come to expect in Holocaust literature. Published as an adult novel in Zusak's native Australia, it was published as YA literature in the United States. It found readers in the YA market, too. Books that can appeal to adults and adolescents and that are accessible to both audiences are rare. This rarity is demonstrative of the rigors of some YA books.

A SOLDIER'S HEART BY GARY PAULSEN

Soldier's Heart (Paulsen 1998), a Civil War novel, is reminiscent of *The Old Man and the Sea* and other classic works. In under a hundred pages, Paulsen is able to recreate for readers the range of emotions felt by our young protagonist, Charlie, as he signs up to play an instrument for one of the regiments from his home town. Charlie begins his duties during the war, excited at the prospect of what he envisions the battles to be. However, soon after being pressed into service as a soldier, Charlie reflects outrage at the carnage he witnesses and, ultimately, resignation at the true horrors of war. What continually confounds me is how Paulsen is able to pack so much into so few pages. By the end of the novel, Charlie possesses a soldier's heart, the condition that today we call posttraumatic stress disorder. Through Charlie's eyes, readers will see the reality and horror of war and bloodshed and death. Reviewers called this novel *spare*, and it is, indeed, a prime example of making each and every word count.

You Don't Know Me by David Klass and *Speak* by Laurie Halse Anderson

Whether you select *You Don't Know Me* (Klass 2002) or *Speak* (Anderson 2000b) does not truly matter. Each delivers the same punch. *You Don't Know Me* is the story of John, a young man who is being secretly abused by his soon-to-be stepfather. *Speak* deals with rape. Both of these books deal with incredibly serious topics and yet both novels contain not insubstantial humorous observations as well. This counterpoint of gravity and humor, which sets up almost a cognitive dissonance, is genius on the part of both Klass and Anderson. What they manage to capture is real life, which is neither constantly hopeless nor constantly a picnic. Instead, life comes at you in waves. Some days are upbeat and wonderful and can turn on a dime and become traumatic. So few books and even fewer authors get that balance right. Klass and Anderson are two who do.

* * *

Reading levels and Lexiles are not the way to determine the rigor of a text. Instead, rigor should be determined by sophistication of thought, depth of character development, stylistic choices, and mastery of language on the part of the author.

I could just as easily have provided a different handful of books to demonstrate the power and richness and wonder that is present in contemporary literature. What I cannot do is talk about reading levels and Lexile levels and how much higher they are. It is true that many YA novels have relatively low reading levels. Lest those who love the canon feel complacent, *Huckleberry Finn* is at the fifth-grade readability level, and *Where the Wild Things Are* is at the fourth-grade level. Reading levels and Lexiles are not the way to determine the rigor of a text. Instead, rigor should be determined by sophistication of thought, depth of character development, stylistic choices, and mastery of language on the part of the author. These are present in the best of YA literature. If they are not present in books your students currently read and enjoy, you can use reading ladders to move them in that direction.

YA's Relevance to Today's Teens

My youngest granddaughter is a junior in high school. One night, she came to me with a question concerning her graphing calculator. Sadly, I told her I could not assist her, as I had never used a graphing calculator (nor a calculator of any kind) when I took math classes. She was, quite frankly, stunned. Her life has always included items such as graphing calculators, iPods, CDs, cell phones, printers, laptop computers, and so much more. I think she sometimes sees me as a sort of dinosaur. All this calls to mind a poem from Mel Glenn's *Class Dismissed!* (1982) in which the narrator, a male teen, asks, Who cares if Willy Loman finds happiness or Moby Dick is ever captured or killed? What do these things have to do with my life? The poem ends with the plaintive query: Got any books that deal with real life?

Dealing with real life: that, in a nutshell, is relevance. Books need to speak to today's readers or they will reject them as not worth reading. Is this something new? Not at all. I recall wondering what some books I was required to read had to do with real life, too, back when I was a teen. When I considered a book to be relevant, it received my full and devoted attention. The same is true for our own students. How did a book become relevant for me? Generally, it was because a teacher or a librarian demonstrated the connection between the book and my life. The goal of this entire book, building reading ladders, is slowly to move students from where they *are* to where we would like them to be. Sometimes I think we forget that beginning with where students *are* is essential. How do we make those connections visible to our students?

First, we can make connections between the themes and topics of books and the lives of our students. Power corrupts; love conquers all; sometimes bad things happen to good people; you can't judge a book by its cover. All of these themes can have connections to students in our classrooms. Finding one's place in the family, getting along with peers, deciding on a career, dealing with parents—these are just a few of the topics that can connect our students to books. YA literature makes the process of connecting books and readers easier because it deals with the challenges and joys of being a teen. *Wintergirls*, by Laurie Halse Anderson (2009), deals with body image and eating disorders. Almost one-third of teen girls deal with some sort of eating disorder during adolescence, according to the latest statistics. *Burn*, by Suzanne Phillips (2008), deals with bullying, specifically what happens when bullies go unchecked. The statistics on bullying are positively stunning. Countless students report being bullied at school with no adult stepping in to assist them. Joan Bauer's *Peeled* (2008) examines what it takes to be a reliable journalist, one that reports rather than invents the news.

Not only are the themes and topics of YA literature relevant, but YA literature has extended the form and format of literature to mirror our students' experience with computers and cell phones and other technology. Text written as IMs and text messages is the form adopted by Lauren Myracle in her novels *Ttyl* (2004), *L8r, G8r* (2007), and *Ttfn* (2006), for instance. Manga appeals to teens who have grown up with Japanese anime as part of their visual world. The increasing presence of graphic novels, including graphic novel (GN) adaptations of classic works, such as *Beowulf* (Hinds 2007) and *The Merchant of Venice* (Hinds 2008), pays heed to the fact that today's teens are prepared for stories in unusual formats.

Making literature relevant does not mean totally dismissing the classics, however. Just as Poe and Hawthorne and Dickens and other authors of what we consider classic literature wrote about the issues and concerns of their own time period, contemporary authors write about the societal issues of today's teens.

Making literature relevant does not mean totally dismissing the classics, however. Just as Poe and Hawthorne and Dickens and other authors of what we consider classic literature wrote about the issues and concerns of their own time period, contemporary authors write about the societal issues of today's teens. Dickens wrote about poverty from his own perspective in history; Sharon Flake, likewise, sets some of her stories in impoverished neighborhoods and talks about the serious circumstances facing kids living in poverty. Poe's horror and mystery stories set the standard for much of what was to follow in those genres. How pleased might he be to read contemporary authors such as Joan Lowery Nixon, whose mysteries made her a four-time winner of the award named for Poe. Or how about Poe reading some of the horror stories collected by Don Gallo in *Short Circuits* (1992)? Hawthorne's *Scarlett Letter* (2009) and Chris Lynch's *Sins of the Fathers* (2006) both rip the veil away from corruption in the church, though the two tackle different sets of circumstances. Making connections between books that our students know and the ones we wish them to read is one way to make reading more relevant.

How can we know which books connect the contemporary to the classic? Certainly, that is one of the thrusts of this book. However, my ultimate goal is to grow and support readers. Sometimes that does not include using literary classics. Other resources are available, though, if you who wish to learn more about contemporary-to-classic connections. Herz and Gallo's *From Hinton to Hamlet* (2005) and Kaywell's *Adolescent Literature as a Complement to the Classics* (2008) are both invaluable resources.

Relevance is not just about connecting contemporary and classic books or about connecting themes and topic or form and format, however. Relevance also means finding books that have other entry points for or connections to readers.

If there is no connection between a text and readers, how can we expect them to enter fully into the story? If the setting is foreign, either because it is in the past or because it is in another country or state or type of neighborhood, then the characters need to have contact points with readers. Thus, we can enter into Kenny and Byron Watson's world in *The Watsons Go to Birmingham—1963* (Curtis 1995), because Kenny and Byron are characters that still resonate with contemporary readers who were not even alive in 1963. Like Kenny and Byron, many readers will connect with the fact that there is sibling rivalry between the younger and older brothers. They will recognize how Byron occasionally takes advantage of his brother and how sweet Kenny's revenge is when Byron does something boneheaded. Some will recognize the embarrassment a family can sometimes cause.

> If there is no connection between a text and readers, how can we expect them to enter fully into the story?

If instead the characters do not resonate with contemporary readers because they are from a different culture, religion, ethnic group, or gender, there can still be touch points between other aspects of the story and readers. For instance, I can read and enjoy *The Outsiders*, by S. E. Hinton (1967), even though I am female. I connect because, like many of the characters, I have felt like an outsider. I did not grow up in Oklahoma (setting), did not belong to a group like the Greasers (character element). But I did long for escape from my neighborhood from time to time. I suspect that I dislike some stories because there are no connection points for me, there is no relevance to me and to my world. Students need a road into the story. So, as you sift through books to be included in your curriculum, ask yourself if there is some route students can take that will permit them access to the book or story.

Some would have us ignore relevance. After all, literature is not about relevance, not about connections to text, not even about the reader. Literature is about meaning, they will argue. Meaning resides within the text, not the reader. As someone who has served on several book selection committees, I have participated in animated discussions about meaning, about character, about theme, about symbolism and much more with colleagues who had all read the same text and yet somehow managed to view it with slightly different lenses. In college courses, it was not unusual to find readings that were required for more than one class. *The Adventures of Huckleberry Finn* was defined by one professor as just a simple story of two people floating down the river on a raft. As you might imagine, another professor saw the book as an important comment on the life and times of Twain, a classic that has stood the test of time, a story that possesses deeper meaning. Literature, it seems, is about more than meaning: it is about what we bring to the reading and how the text connects to us as readers. Perhaps the discussion on the nature of response will be one answer to those who would dismiss relevance so easily.

The Relationships YA Can Build and Sustain

Teens seek relationships. Recall that during this time, few teens elect to be on their own. Instead, they travel in packs, cliques, groups. They reach beyond their communities to those they can find online—MySpace, Facebook, Second Life, Twitter, and others. Books can also build and sustain relationships.

Recently, my husband found me sobbing over a book. "What's wrong? Why are you crying?" He was truly concerned that someone had phoned with bad news or I was somehow hurt. Once I could gather myself together, I told him that my crying was a result of the book I was reading. *Deadline* (2007), by Chris Crutcher, caused me to sob aloud at several different points. How did this happen? I think it is because YA literature can create empathy. Empathy, stronger than sympathy, connects to the reader at a deep emotional level. Something in the book has happened to the reader as well; thus, a relationship is made, one that can be sustained book by book. When I listen to Jack Gantos narrate his Joey Pigza books, the same sort of relationship is made. Here, in essence, is Jack reading his book aloud to me personally. The next time a Gantos book comes my way, I am more likely to pick it up and read it because he has become part of my social network through that first connection.

Lifetime readers have developed relationships with books and authors. We prowl the bookstores seeking the latest offerings from favorites we have come to know. A quick glance at the best-seller list certainly reinforces this concept; week after week, the list contains familiar names: King, Clancy, Baldacci, Higgins Clark, and Picoult, to list a few. Turn to the list of children's best sellers and the names are just as familiar: Prelutsky, Silverstein, Willems, Scieszka, and Selznick, among others. (And now it is easy to see names cross from the adult list to the one for younger readers: James Patterson and Sherman Alexie are just two of the authors who publish works in both adult and children's venues.) So, if we are to be about the business of creating lifetime readers and not just readers who can utilize phonological awareness and context clues to bubble in answers on a state test, then we need to help our students form those relationships with books and authors and genres and formats.

How we can connect kids to book after book after book is at the heart of *this* book. It is not a simple task. It is, though, one of the most rewarding tasks we can perform with our students. Reading ladders can help us do this well.

The Neglected R: Response

As soon as I say "neglected," I immediately wonder if that is really the correct adjective here. What has masqueraded as response, especially in the era of high-stakes testing, bears little resemblance to the meaning of the word as intentioned by scholars such as Louise Rosenblatt and Robert Probst. In many classrooms, response has been reduced to multiple-choice questions answered on a computer or the five-paragraph essay replete with theses sentences that state not what students think about their reading but rather what someone else has told them to think. *Neglected*, then, might indicate that students are not being asked to respond to text. That's not entirely true; what I mean to say is that many of these programmed responses are not in the least concerned with authenticity.

Rosenblatt and Probst would define authentic response differently. For them, response can take many forms. It can be our first gut reaction to what we read—a personal and emotional response. Response could also take the form of a more measured response, one that we arrive at after some reflection and perhaps some guiding questions. Authentic response also demands that, as teachers, we do not possess a correct answer or *the* interpretation of a piece of literature. Rather, with students, we should arrive at a negotiated answer or interpretation. And, more important, we should help students become independent so that they can navigate texts and produce responses even when we are not there to assist them. Therefore, helping students become more independent is also one of the chief aims of reading ladders as described in this book.

*   *   *

As I completed the initial draft of this chapter, I was looking out at the city of Atlanta spread below me. I was there for the International Reading Association's conference of 2008. The night before, two colleagues sat in that hotel room, and we pored over the convention program. We dog-eared pages with the sessions we most wanted to attend. Many of them had authors as speakers; some focused on the role of books to motivate readers. For almost an entire week, thousands of my friends and colleagues celebrated books and reading. Later, as I revised this book, I was freshly returned from the National Council of Teachers of English conference in San Antonio. I watched a room that would hold more than eight hundred people fill and then overflow as participants flooded in to listen to Greg Mortenson. I saw a record crowd come to the ALAN (Assembly on Literature for Adolescents of NCTE) two-day workshop after the conference to listen to more than fifty YA authors talk about books and reading and writing.

I know many of us are searching continually for that just-right book for each and every one of our students. It is my sincere hope that this book will assist you in finding the right books for your students. More importantly, I hope that this book will also help you guide your students to the *next* great book and the one after that and so on. That is the purpose of reading ladders. It is not sufficient to find just one book for each reader; we need to be able to guide that reader toward other books. It is time now to venture forward into the wide and wonderful world of books. We need to discover how we can, in turn, set our students' feet upon the path we will tread first: the path that leads to lifetime reading and lifelong learning.

Lincoln Logs

How We Begin to Build Lifelong Readers

One of my eighth-grade students once remarked that he thought I sprang from my mother's womb with a book in hand, reading. Not quite. However, I was a reader early in life. I know that there are several factors that started me off on the road to lifelong reading. I also understand that my own experiences were not unique. I have witnessed them in my own home as I've reared two generations of lifelong readers and in my own classroom—from the prekindergarten children I worked with, to the middle school students with whom I spent a great deal of time as a teacher, to the graduate students who populate my classes today. These factors are the Lincoln Logs of reading, the sturdy foundational pieces that are necessary in the development of lifelong reading. Let's take a moment and review them here as a foundation for the rest of this book.

Foundational Piece 1: Reading Aloud

Forming a sturdy foundation requires being read aloud to along the way. My first strong memory of reading is my grandfather (we called him PopPop) sharing *Pat the*

Bunny (Kunhardt 1940) with me. I was sitting in his lap, and I still recall touching the scrap of sandpaper on the page that said Paul and Judy could touch Daddy's scratchy face. Whenever I pick up that book today, I catch a whiff of the special powder PopPop used. That strong almost physical memory reminds me of how powerful this simple act can be in the development of lifetime readers.

Reading aloud for fifteen minutes a day at least three times a week is foundational in building lifelong readers (Trelease 2006).

As an educator, I have now read the research on the importance of reading aloud. I know that reading aloud can affect not only attitudes toward books and reading but growth in reading ability. Reading aloud for fifteen minutes a day at least three times a week is foundational in building lifelong readers (Trelease 2006). A meta-analysis of the effects of reading aloud was conducted decades ago and showed that students who were read aloud to on a regular basis scored higher on tests of word usage, vocabulary, and reading comprehension. Their attitudes toward books and reading were more positive as well (Martinez 1989). It saddens me to see that reading aloud has become something of a luxury in this era of No Child Left Behind, where once children become independent readers, some educators feel there is no further need for this activity. Later in this book, I examine this simple act and explore why it needs to remain the cornerstone of a literacy-rich environment.

Foundational Piece 2: Access to Books

In order for a reading foundation to be strong, it must include access to books. My mother made sure I got a library card as soon as I was old enough and would take me to the Carnegie Library to check out books every couple of weeks. Books were my favorite presents for Christmas and other occasions. Having ready access to books in the home, in school, or at the library is essential. Without access to books, how can a habit, let alone a love, of reading develop? Natalie, my youngest granddaughter, demanded we take her to the public library on her fifth birthday, as she could finally get her *own* library card. She had plenty of books in the house and could always count on someone to buy her a book whenever she wanted something new to read, but to her a library card was akin to a driver's license: it was an entrée to a special club. She could now spend hours browsing the shelves of the library.

As a middle school teacher, I understood the importance of regular visits to the school library. For many of my students, the books in my classroom and in the school library were the only reading materials they had access to. This is, sadly, still the case for many of our students; my work with a local school confirms that access to books within the home is still limited for many students. When we asked students at this campus how many books they had at home (we did a simple survey every year with students in grades 7–12), the median answer was two. That so intrigued me that I did some follow-up interviews to determine which two books were in the homes. The fact that one of the books was the Bible was not surprising. However, the second book most often mentioned by students was the telephone book.

Stephen Krashen (2008) notes the importance of access to books as well when he posits that access to books is a better predictor of success in school than other factors, such as socioeconomic status. Access, then, is another Lincoln Log added to the foundation. More discussion about classroom, school, and public libraries appears throughout this book, especially in Chapter 3.

Foundational Piece 3: Models of Literacy

If we are to develop as lifelong readers, having models of literacy around us can be key. My mother was what we would now term an avid reader. To me, she was just Mom. Despite the fact that she worked outside of the house, I saw her engaged in literate behavior on a regular basis. Even at the end of a long day at work, Mom would curl up with a book or magazine and read at bedtime. She had *True Confessions* and other materials on the table next to her bed. She wrote notes on all her Christmas cards to update friends and family on the events of the past year. She proofread my term papers in college. Up until her death, she still read *Reader's Digest* and worked crossword puzzles when she could not sleep.

This is where my life as a reader and writer began. My husband and I are seldom without a book. It should be no surprise, then, that our children and grandchildren are avid readers. My daughter turned to romance novels as an escape from chemotherapy. She would spend hours hooked up to an IV, deeply engrossed in the latest tome featuring the coiffed Fabio and some damsel in distress on the cover. Her children use books to escape as well: to escape from the tedium of the literary canon, to escape from the summer reruns on TV, to escape from each other.

As a teacher, I ensure that my students see me engaged in reading and writing. When I worked with middle school students, I read along with them during silent reading time at school. I talked to them about the books I was reading. When I moved to the university classroom, I continued to model the behaviors I expected from my students. I read aloud in class, talked about my own reading, wrote samples of all their assignments, and even composed in front of the class to show students my process. For the past seven years, in addition to reading and talking about books and reading, I have maintained a blog about my reading (professornana.livejournal.com/) and included booklists at my website (www.professornana.com/). I hope to stay a model, even if it is sometimes just a digital model. The third Lincoln Log, then, is having models of literacy present in the lives of children.

Foundational Piece 4: Time to Read

Reading aloud, access to books, and models of literacy will mean little in terms of developing readers unless there is *time* for them to actually read. It is helpful to think of time spent reading within a sports metaphor. Anyone involved in a sport from amateur to professional can attest that practice makes perfect. Look at the hours our students spend at football and volleyball and soccer practice. Are they sitting inside the gym listening to someone explain a quarterback sneak or a set-and-spike or bunt? More likely, the players are out on the field actually practicing these techniques. The same should hold true for reading.

> Reading aloud, access to books, and models of literacy will mean little in terms of developing readers unless there is *time* for them to actually read.

I discovered early on in my teaching that setting aside time for students to read silently every day at school was important. I had no control over my students' time once they were out of school, but I could carve out some time for them to read in my classroom. Moreover, I could control the classroom environment so that reading was more likely to occur. Quiet; adequate lighting; access to books; places to curl up with books; and a model of reading (that would be me): these are essential components of a successful environment for silent reading. Nancie Atwell, Linda Rief, Kylene Beers, and so many other educators have noted the importance of silent reading inside the school day. In this time of No Child Left Behind, some classrooms have lost this time for reading. How can we convince others that it is a component that needs to be re-instated? Here are a few valid points to raise in the discussion.

Time spent actually reading is more than simply practice. Students who read more know more about story grammar, or how a story is constructed. Ask a child who has read quite a bit to tell you a story, and you will see immediately that she knows how to construct one. There is a beginning (often "Once upon a time," which indicates setting, too), a middle where events are linked causally ("and then . . . and then . . . and then"), and an ending ("and they lived happily ever after. The End."). On the surface, this might seem a tad simplistic. However, think about the power of this story grammar when it comes time not only to tell a story but to write one, often for one of our many state-mandated tests.

We know that students who read more have a larger vocabulary. I have witnessed this over and over in conversations with students, even my own teens. One year, we took the kids to the Renaissance festival outside of town. As we were walking along, Natalie, then aged eleven, commented that the smell of the fried ice cream was "wafting" through the air and inviting her to come and have some. Forget that she pronounced the word incorrectly (she said it was WAYF-ting). We could correct that. She knew the word and its meaning sufficiently to use it. In the classroom, I see students use words I know they have encountered in their recreational reading. They are not words we have discussed in class, nor are they words likely heard out in the hallways. Instead, they are the words they have encountered in texts. Words like *morose*, from one of the Lemony Snicket books (which are models for teaching students about context clues, by the way, since Snicket generally follows up the use of one of these words with a sentence that explains its meaning), or the "word of the day" battle between the main characters of *A Northern Light*, by Jennifer Donnelly (2003), can build vocabulary in a way that seems effortless to most readers.

Additionally, the more time students spend engaged in books and reading, the more likely this practice is to extend beyond the walls of the classroom. The more time they spend engaged in reading, especially recreational or pleasure reading, the more motivated students are to read for more extensive periods of time—that means more books, longer books, or more complex books. And, finally, remembering that practice makes perfect: the more students read, the more easily they read. Fluency and prosody are not automatic, of course, but they are enhanced by more time spent reading.

* * *

These seemingly simple things—hearing books read aloud, having access to books, seeing models of literacy, having time to read—went a long way toward forming my reading habits and even my earliest preferences. Readers are made, not born. The experiences we present students can have terrific influence, sometimes more than we can see at the time. Also, I think it is important to note here that children and teens who come to class with a myriad of such experiences in their background are more likely to be our avid readers.

Unfortunately, the reverse is also true. I know there are homes without books; homes where there are not models of reading; homes where reading aloud is not a nightly occurrence; homes where time is not set aside for reading. I remember Cali, now twenty-three, in middle school telling her friends that she had met Gary Paulsen. She was literally floating on air when she met Paulsen and had the chance to have her book signed. Her friends were less than impressed, and when she gave autographed books as gifts at birthday parties: the reception was considerably less enthused than when she gave them at home. Cali learned, as did her sisters who followed, that not everyone loved books and reading the way we did. Do those children and teens, the ones for whom books and reading are not exciting experiences, come to class with the same expectations? How can they?

Don't take my word. There is plenty of research out there that confirms that readers are formed out of their experiences. For me, the quintessential work is that of Anne Sherrill and G. Robert Carlsen. In *Voices of Readers: How We Come to Love Books*, Sherrill and Carlsen (1988) offer suggestions about those common experiences that form us early on as readers as well as other experiences from our later life of reading that are essential. At the outset of each semester, the students in my young adult literature classes write their reading autobiographies. This assignment was one I found incredibly informative when I took YA literature from Dr. Richard Abrahamson. His mentor, Dr. Robert Carlsen, required the same assignment of Dick. Now, as I read the assignments submitted by my students, I am struck by the commonalities. My students range not only in age and experience but also in professional settings; I have teachers from the Rio Grande Valley of Texas, educators in small towns in east Texas, and people who work with students in inner-city schools in Houston. What most of them have in common, however, is a love of books and reading. This is what has led them to our program: they want to become school librarians. Why do they so love books and reading? Their reading autobiographies mention the same common features presented by Sherrill and Carlsen in *Voices of Readers*: being read aloud to by parents or teachers, having access to books at home or through public and school libraries, seeing models of literacy at home or at school. Simply talking to readers will confirm most of the research as well. Ask the teachers you admire as literacy educators about their memories of reading as children, teens, adults. Chances are they will respond with similar answers: reading aloud, access to books, models of literacy, time to read.

Other research by educators from the '60s to the current day not only confirms Sherrill and Carlsen's research but also offers additional suggestions for those who work with reluctant readers. The working metaphor for this chapter has been Lincoln Logs—toys that provide the basic tools for constructing objects. Over the years, I have watched as Lincoln Logs were refined and reimagined into Tinker Toys and, eventually, Legos. Even Legos are being improved upon with the next generation of flexible building materials that represent a broader potential for construction. In other words, these toys and their potential for building have moved from those basic building blocks (Lincoln Logs) to materials that could build up and out from the foundation more easily (Tinker Toys) to materials that could turn corners and move in different directions (Legos). I think what we know about motivating readers fits into this analogy. We have moved from the basics (reading aloud, access to books, models of literacy, and time to read) to refined and reimagined concepts and techniques (higher levels of thinking about texts, such as analysis and synthesis and evaluation) to even more ingenious materials, strategies, and techniques that embrace alternative views of the same text and support a variety of ways to respond to reading (reader response, thinking through text). So, consider this analogy as the structure for this book: we begin with the basics, move to the reimagined, and continue on to the ingenious.

If you have watched children explore these building materials, you know that, at first, they struggle. Sometimes they attempt to build something without an adequate foundation. At other times, they do not know how to move from the foundation to the next level of the building. They get frustrated and simply quit, occasionally knocking over their work. And so it goes with readers. They need an adequate foundation, they need to know how to build upon that foundation, and they need our assistance when things get so frustrating that they are tempted to simply surrender. It is my hope that this book assists all of us as we guide readers toward a lifelong love of books and reading.

A Final Thought on Building Readers

I am a huge fan of the Food Network. I do not have the panache of an Emeril Lagasse or the knife skills of a Rachel Ray. And as much as I love *Iron Chef*, I never envision myself in Kitchen Stadium wielding pots and pans with Mario Batali. No, I watch the shows for two reasons. First, they are a terrific escape from the work that always seems to await me. Second and more important, I watch them to gather ideas for my own cooking. My skills have slowly improved, and I am more tempted to take risks when I cook as a result of my growing confidence. So, if you will pardon me for inserting another analogy here, I think confidence that grows gradually through observation, trial and error, and eventual risk taking and success is a key for motivating and encouraging readers as well. And let me extend this metaphor one step further: just as I watch the Food Network and garner ideas about cooking and meal planning, I hope this book serves as a place to gather ideas for all of us to try. It is my wish that readers take any information in this book and make it work in their own classrooms. After all, for that to happen successfully, we each need to tweak its ideas and suggestions until they work with our own students.

When I read Nancie Atwell's *In the Middle* (1998), I remember feeling somehow vindicated that much of what I was doing with students in my own classroom was described in that groundbreaking book. I also adopted some of her other strategies and activities. Occasionally, of course, an idea I tried did not work for me in my own classroom. And the first time I attempted Harvey Daniels' literature circles (see, for example, Daniels 2002 and Daniels and Steineke 2004)? Those poor students are probably still in therapy! Were these failures the fault of Atwell and Daniels? Of course not. I attempted to take their ideas and simply plop them down into my class without thinking about the differences between my students and theirs, my school and theirs, the structure of my classroom and theirs.

Adapt the strategies, techniques, and activities to meet the individual needs of your students and classes and school.

So, use this book as a starting point. Remember that each of us has a unique classroom situation and a unique classroom presence. Adapt the strategies, techniques, and activities to meet the individual needs of your students and classes and school. Adapt, tweak, fiddle to your heart's content. Then, share your experiences with your colleagues. Talk about the successes and failures. It might require adding some ingredients and removing or substituting others. That's OK. This is not *the* recipe for success in building lifelong readers. I hope it is, instead, a solid plan for tapping into the passion we all have for books and reading and creating that same passion in all of our students.

Motivating Readers

Motivation is a key element in the success of any endeavor. Whether it is dieting or breaking a bad habit or doing well in school, success relies in large part on our motivation. It is important to note that real motivation is intrinsic, coming from *within* readers. Motivation from without, extrinsic motivation, can work *if* the reward being offered is of value to the recipient of your efforts. Remove that reward or incentive, and the behavior being rewarded often ceases. Moreover, extrinsic motivation does not morph magically into intrinsic motivation. Since there is not a prize for those adults who buy the most books at the bookstore or those who check out the most books from the library, students who grew up with only extrinsic motivation may not transform into adult readers.

Think of motivation as the beginning of a cycle that prompts engagement; its key components are action and practice, which in turn prompt success, which refuels motivation. Figure 3.1 illustrates this positive and beneficial cycle.

So, what motivates students to read? The simplest way to answer this question is to ask the students themselves. A variety of researchers have done just that for

Figure 3.1 *The Cycle of Motivation*

decades. Over and over again, three variables produce the strongest effect: book variables, student variables, and school variables.

Book Variables

What variables affect how students select books? Have you watched students in the process of selecting books? Sometimes it appears so random. How are they making decisions? What made Naomi pick up *Make Lemonade* by Virginia Euwer Wolff (1993), when a few of her friends walked past the same book without a glance or pause? How did Juan decide that *The Whole Sky Full of Stars* (Saldaña 2007) would be a book he might like to read? Is the process of book selection so idiosyncratic that each student selects a book in a different way from his classmates? Are there some commonalities?

After many hours of observation, I began to notice certain consistent factors that seem to contribute to selection. But why not go directly to the source? With that in mind, I designed a simple survey and asked the students what went into their deliberations. Class after class, year after year, similar factors emerged, and my own university students confirm that these factors are still in play. Even my colleagues with whom I have served on book selection committees reaffirmed this bit of field research. Here, then, is a list of the factors that play some sort of role in book selection.

- **Title:** Is the title compelling? Does it promise mystery or intrigue or suspense or humor?
- **Cover:** How is color used? Are the colors bold or muted? What about the illustrations or pictures? Do they cause a reader to pause and look again?
- **Opening paragraph:** Does the author capture the reader in those first couple of sentences? What hooks are being used?

- **Form and format:** Is the book unusual and, therefore, set apart from the others? Is it a graphic novel or manga? Are chapters short? Is there white space on each page?

- **Genre:** Do students tend to pick up certain types of books? Is nonfiction a draw? Are vampire stories still hot?

- **Style:** Does this book demonstrate a distinct style of writing, one different from most books?

The Triumvirate: Title, Cover, and Opening Text

Title, cover, and opening paragraph are the triumvirate, the elements that must grab students first if the other factors are even going to have a chance. Factors such as form, format, genre, and style are important, of course, and are discussed a bit later. Before my service on the committee to revise *Books for You* (Beers and Lesesne 2001) and *Your Reading* (Brown 2003), before three years spent deliberating books with the rest of the Quick Picks for Reluctant Readers committee or on the Children's Choices Committee, I might have included other variables, such as length or readability. While those can play some slight role and are mentioned later in this chapter, they can't compare with the role played by title, cover, and opening paragraphs or chapter.

> Title, cover, and opening paragraph are the triumvirate, the elements that must grab students first if the other factors are even going to have a chance.

Title

Take a look at the titles in Table 3.1. If you presented students with only the titles of the books listed there, which do you think they would elect to read?

I suspect that many readers would select some of the same titles including *Night of the Homework Zombies* (Nickel 2006), *Dead Is the New Black* (Perez 2008),

TITLES THAT GRAB STUDENT READERS	
Fever, 1793	*42 Miles*
How to Steal a Dog	*Ghostgirl*
Dead Is the New Black	*Generation Dead*
Into the Volcano	*Paper Towns*
Evernight	*Burn*
Underwear: What We Wear Under There	*Night of the Homework Zombies*
Supernatural Rubber Chicken: Fowl Language	*Night Road*
Madapple	*Sunrise over Fallujah*
The Mysterious Benedict Society	*How to Get Suspended and Influence People*
The London Eye Mystery	

Table 3.1 *Titles that Grab Student Readers*

Ghostgirl (Hurley 2008), *Generation Dead* (Waters 2008), *Supernatural Rubber Chicken: Fowl Language* (Garfinkle 2008), and perhaps *How to Steal a Dog* (O'Connor 2007) or *How to Get Suspended and Influence People* (Selzer 2006). What do these titles have in common? In some cases, there is a hint of mystery, such as *How to Get Suspended and Influence People* and *How to Steal a Dog*. There are titles that seem to promise some humor, most notably *Supernatural Rubber Chicken: Fowl Language* and *Night of the Homework Zombies*. Finally, there are titles that indicate potentially dark content: *Dead Is the New Black*, *Generation Dead*, and *Ghostgirl*. Conduct your own experiment here. Browse the *New York Times* best-seller list, the "Best Books for Young Adults" list, or the "Quick Picks for Reluctant Readers" list and note twenty or so titles on a simple survey. Ask your students to select the books they would most like to read based solely on the titles. Do titles influence them?

If I were working with a group of reluctant readers and simply displayed the books listed in Table 3.1 for browsing, I think the titles mentioned here would be picked up quickly. Does that mean that the other titles would not appeal to readers? Not at all. The remainder of these titles would soon be selected based on their covers or their opening paragraphs. That is why these three variables form what I am calling the triumvirate.

Cover

In this time of consumerism, when manufacturers target children knowing if they capture consumers at a young age, they will have loyal consumers for decades to come, it is no wonder that publishers know the value of cover art when it comes to attracting potential readers. Students do rely on covers when selecting books. As Melissa Potter, chair of the Voice of Youth Advocates Top Shelf Fiction for Middle School Readers project, observed, "Middle school students absolutely do judge books by their covers. If the characters on a book's front cover looked too young or the artwork looked too amateurish, the teens would not read it—even with pushing" (2009, 490).

Drawing from the list in Table 3.1, certain books will attract readers based on their covers. *Evernight* (Gray 2008) and *Night Road* (Jenkins 2008) are both dark covers that promise stories about vampires. The cover of *Underwear: What We Wear Under There* (Swain 2008) has, well, underwear on the cover. *Into the Volcano* (Wood 2008) holds out the promise of action and adventure in its graphic novel format. The cover of *Madapple* (Meldrum 2008), with its picture of a young woman whose hair frames her face in twisted strands, is intriguing; the colors are muted with hints of darkness, which seems to promise some sort of ancient magic (and the book does deliver on that promise). Walter Dean Myers' *Sunrise over Fallujah* (2008b), with its cover in shades of red and orange and soldiers in battle gear, lets readers know a little about its contents before they turn one page. Might all the other covers attract as well? Certainly this is possible. Students come to us with a wide range of experiences and interests. Only by listening to and observing them can we begin to zero in on the titles and covers that appeal.

Opening Paragraphs or Chapter

We have come a long way from, "It was a dark and stormy night." However, despite the distance we have traveled, there is still a bit of the hook evident in the books that appeal to the less than avid readers in our classes. And that brings us to the remaining titles from the table: *Fever, 1793* (Anderson 2000a), *The Mysterious Benedict Society* (Stewart 2007), *42 Miles* (Zimmer 2008), *Paper Towns* (Green 2008), and *Burn* (Phillips 2008). While these books might have cover and title appeal among some readers, if we take a few minutes to read aloud from the opening pages of each of these books, we'll find they will sell themselves. Authors know they must entice readers to enter into the world they are creating or re-creating. That invitation can come in a variety of forms.

- In *Fever, 1793*, sixteen-year-old Mattie is confronted with the usual problems of a teen in the eighteenth century. However, before long, Mattie's life takes a turn as the yellow fever epidemic threatens all the residents of Mattie's town. What begins with a hint of Laurie Halse Anderson's hallmark wit and understanding of the teen life in any time period soon becomes a story of survival with harrowing close calls.

- *The Mysterious Benedict Society*, by Trenton Lee Stewart, presents a young boy named Reynie who answers an ad for gifted students willing to take a test for a special school. The rules for entering into the test site are bizarre (only one pencil and eraser, must be on time), but the test itself is even stranger. The lure of the unknown and unexpected will draw readers into this middle-grade mystery.

- John Green's *Paper Towns* promises adventure and potential romance along with a mystery. In the middle of the night, Margo Roth Spiegelman entices neighbor and childhood friend Quentin Jacobsen to accompany her on a secret mission. She, dressed as a ninja, is plotting sweet revenge, and Quentin is eager to be in her company again since he has harbored a crush on her for a long time. Who could resist following Quentin into a maze of clues and red herrings in this YA novel?

- *42 Miles* is a novel in verse. This intimate glimpse into the life of JoEllen, who divides her week between her mother's apartment in the city and her father's family farm in the country, invites readers from the first entry, which explains JoEllen's rather schizophrenic life with two separate identities.

GREET OPENING PASSAGES	
Middle School	**High School**
The Tale of Desperaux (DiCamillo 2003)	*The Adoration of Jenna Fox* (Pearson 2008)
Masterpiece (Broach 2008)	*Soul Enchilada* (Gill 2009)
The Mostly True Adventures of Homer P. Figg (Philbrick 2009)	*Wintergirls* (Anderson 2009)
Everything Is Fine (Ellis 2009)	*Eternal* (Smith 2009)
	This Full House (Wolff 2009)
Scat (Hiaasen 2009)	*Would You* (Jocelyn 2008)
The Underneath (Appelt 2008)	*Black Rabbit Summer* (Brooks 2008)
Nation (Pratchett 2008)	*Little Brother* (Doctorow 2008)
The Graveyard Book (Gaiman 2008b)	*Skinned* (Wasserman 2008)
My One Hundred Adventures (Horvath 2008)	*Absolutely Maybe* (Yee 2009)
Geek Chic: The Zoey Zone (Palatini 2008)	

Table 3.2 *Great Opening Passages*

> They try to split me
> like an apple's pale heart
> on either side of the blade
> pretending
> my life is like
> Mr. Howard's hexagon,
> equal parts
> no matter
> how many times they cut it. (Zimmer 2008, 7)

- *Burn*, by Suzanne Phillips, gives readers the story of a troubled, bullied teen named Cameron. Since the first day of his freshman year, Cameron has been subjected to torture from the Red Coats, the jocks who sport red athletic jackets. The attacks are mean and quick and under the radar of the adults (or so it would seem). Readers will react, as I did, with outrage at this torment and feel as helpless as Cameron himself.

Frequently, I use books with riveting opening passages for quick booktalks with classes of students. Reading aloud a paragraph, a poem, or a short chapter can often create some powerful motivation for students. Table 3.2 includes some other titles whose opening passages might just lure some of the most reluctant readers in your classrooms.

Booktalking is discussed in more detail in Chapter 4, but developing the habit of looking at books as our students do is an important one. Examining the cover and title and reading the opening passages are quick and simple activities that can help us connect readers to books almost instantaneously.

FORM, FORMAT, GENRE, AND STYLE

Once they pick up a book, what makes kids read it? Though the preceding factors bear weight in book selection among adolescents, there are some other factors that can play a role. A unique format, such as a graphic novel or novel in verse, can make a student pause, peruse, *read*. Genre can be a deciding factor, too; students often become enamored of a certain genre and read that exclusively for weeks or even months. Mysteries are popular, for instance, as are nonfiction and fantasy. Most students have a favorite. Characterizing a book by naming its genre can get some students interested before they've even seen the cover. Style, the most elusive of the factors, is intensely subjective, but don't discount its impact. This is often what makes a reader a loyal fan of a single author. Let's take a closer look at these influential factors.

Form and Format

Have you noticed the preponderance of new books that are in graphic novel format? GNs, as they are known, used to occupy a small niche of the YA market. Now, they seem to have become more mainstream and more widely available. *American Born Chinese*, by Gene Yang (2006), became the first GN to win the prestigious Printz Award, given for distinguished contribution to literature for young adults. The Young Adult Library Services Association of the American Library Association (YALSA) now offers an annual "Great Graphic Novels for Teens" list (for information on the YALSA lists and awards, visit www.ala.org/yalsa/). Japanese anime influence is evident in manga, a format similar to graphic novels. More recently, GN versions of popular novels have surfaced, such as *Coraline*, by Neil Gaiman (2008a), the Artemis Fowl books (Colfer), and the animal fantasies of Brian Jacques. GN versions of classics, especially *Beowulf* and *The Merchant of Venice*, both by Gareth Hinds (2007, 2008), and Peter Kuper's *Metamorphosis* (2003), demonstrate the growth of this format. Table 3.3 lists some graphic novels you might want to peruse and add to your collections.

In addition to the aforementioned formats, picture books for older readers continue to extend this form beyond elementary grades. The success of *The Wall*, by Peter Sís (2007), and *The Arrival*, by Shaun Tan (2007), and other award-winning books has ensured that older readers will find picture books that not only interest them but are appropriate for them. Picture books can deal with a diverse range of topics—suicide, Communism, immigration, and so much more—within a format that makes the ideas accessible for readers who might struggle with longer and more complex texts. The scaffolding that illustrations, pictures, charts, graphs, and maps can provide enhances and elaborates the text. In an era where visual and media

GRAPHIC NOVELS	
Beowulf (Hinds 2007)	*Kin* (Black 2008)
Garage Band (Gipi 2007)	*Rapunzel's Revenge* (Hale 2008)
Laika (Abadzis 2007)	*The Plain Janes* (Castellucci 2007)
Merchant of Venice (Hinds 2008)	*Malcolm X: A Graphic Biography* (Helfer 2006)
American Born Chinese (Yang 2006)	*Houdini: The Handcuff King* (Lutes 2007)
Gettysburg (Butzer 2009)	*Stuck in the Middle: Seventeen Comics from an Unpleasant Age* (Schrag 2007)
Pedro and Me (Winick 2000)	*The 911 Report: A Graphic Adaptation* (Jacobson and Colon 2006)
Bone (Smith 1994)	
Maus I and *Maus II* (Spiegelman 1986 and 1992)	*To Dance: A Ballerina's Graphic Novel* (Siegel 2006)
The United States Constitution: A Graphic Adaptation (Hennessey 2008)	*Kristy's Great Idea* (Martin and Telgemeier 2006)
	Light Brigade (Tomasi 2005)
Life Sucks (Abel and Soria 2007)	*Swallow Me Whole* (Powell 2008)
Skim (Tamaki 2008)	

Table 3.3 *Graphic Novels*

literacy is considered crucial, the picture book can offer much reward for classroom use.

Where can you locate picture books for older readers? Try looking at the books that win the Caldecott Award from the Association for Library Service to Children (ALSC), a division of the American Library Association (www.ala.org/alsc/). *Flotsam*, a textless picture book by David Wiesner (2006), for instance, presents an opportunity for even those with limited reading skills to participate in a reading. *Jumanji*, by Chris Van Allsburg (1981), offers lessons in perspective and point of view. Peter Sís' *Starry Messenger* (2006) is nonfiction; *Lon Po Po*, by Ed Young (1989), gives readers a variation of the Red Riding Hood story; and Mordecai Gerstein's *Man Who Walked Between the Towers* (2003) could be used to compare book with movie, as the documentary of Phillipe Petit's daredevil tightrope walk between the World Trade Center towers is now available on DVD.

Another form that has taken a place of prominence in the field is the novel in verse. Though the Newbery-winning *Out of the Dust*, by Karen Hesse (1997), brought critical attention to the form, it had already existed in YA literature for some time. The work of Mel Glenn in novels such as *The Taking of Room 114* (1997) and *Foreign Exchange* (1999) are terrific examples of how this form works, how individual poems create characters and advance the plot. Ellen Hopkins' stunning *Identical* (2008) and *Glass* (2007) provide intense reads for teen girls in particular. Sonya Sones has used this form in *What My Mother Doesn't Know* (2001) and *Stop*

Pretending (1999). *The Surrender Tree*, by Margarita Engle (2008), relates the story of Cuba's struggle for freedom in poems that span decades of history. Virginia Euwer Wolff's trilogy *Make Lemonade* (1993), *True Believer* (2001), and *This Full House* (2009) follow the same main character from her early to late teens. And while many of these titles have a largely female audience, there are some books that appeal to the guys as well, including the aforementioned Mel Glenn titles. David Levithan's *Realm of Possibility* (2006) is a complex novel in verse with multiple voices, many of them male. What is it about this form that attracts readers? Librarian Lois Buckman suggests that part of the appeal is the appearance of the text on the page. One of her library patrons, a very reluctant reader, confided, "There are, like, not so many words as in these other books. And, look, these books are shorter, too. It's all good, right?"

Genre

How does genre affect book selection? For decades, researchers have asked students to identify the reading genres they prefer. What genres appeal to students? Ask. Again, a simple survey can provide information about the books your students prefer in terms of genre. (See Chapter 5 for a sample student survey.) My own research over the past twenty-five years has concluded that, while some genres wax and wane in terms of popularity, there are a few that remain favorites. Mysteries and nonfiction always come to the forefront when I ask students to select from a list of genres. Fantasy is also currently enjoying popularity, helped along over the past decade by the enormous success of the Harry Potter saga. Since classes and students differ from year to year (and sometimes from moment to moment), asking your own classes is the best method of determining which books to add to your collection.

Style

Style is perhaps the most difficult element to pin down. Often, students are not terribly conversant about style: they realize that there is something about a particular author that appeals to them, but they do not always possess the vocabulary to discuss what that elusive something is. Occasionally, style preferences are tied to some of the other variables, most notably genre. Mysteries are popular in part because of the way in which the author reveals the clues that assist the reader in solving the puzzle. Nonfiction may be popular because it conveys information in a variety of forms: through text, illustrations, graphs, and other visual media. A student who read fantasy told Kylene Beers once that reading fantasy was like "floating on the breath of a cloud." That escapist nature of fantasy is something that appeals to many readers.

Student Variables

Most often mentioned in a discussion of student variables are age, gender, and intelligence. In actuality, only one of these variables plays an essential role for tweens and teens: gender. Certainly when students are in elementary grades, age plays a role. Readers move from picture books to early chapter books and finally to novels. Interestingly, now that the YA world has entered into an age where graphic novels are part of the mainstream offerings, one could almost argue that we are returning to the picture book, an entity that tells a story in words and in pictures. However, the chronological age of a reader is less of a variable than the developmental age of the reader, a point I discuss later. Intelligence or ability is not an overriding variable either. Most eighth graders, be they struggling or gifted, are looking for similar things in books. Form, format, genre, and style (all book variables) might constitute either impediment or assistance, depending on reading ability. However, it is the gender of the reader that presents the biggest obstacles when selecting books for students.

I know that this is an emotionally charged issue. Recently, an article in a Boston newspaper decried that gender differences did not truly exist and that boys and girls would read the same books if only they were offered them. However, more than a decade of experience in working with middle school students directly, and another couple of decades of talking about books with a wide range of students across the country, confirms that gender differences *do* exist.

Take a look at the book titles in Table 3.4 and see if you can determine which ones will appeal more to boys than girls.

GENDER-BASED TITLES
Dead Is the New Black
Encyclopedia Horrifica
Ghostgirl
Knucklehead
Love Me Tender
North of Beautiful
On the Wings of Heroes
Regarding the Bathrooms
The Adoration of Jenna Fox
The Boy Who Dared
The Earth, My Butt, and Other Big Round Things
What Buttosaur Is That?

Table 3.4 *Gender-Based Titles*

Some of the selections are no-brainers. *What Buttosaur Is That?* (Griffiths 2008), *Regarding the Bathrooms* (Klise 2006), *Knucklehead* (Scieszka 2008), *The Boy Who Dared* (Bartoletti 2008), *On the Wings of Heroes* (Peck 2007), and *Encyclopedia Horrifica* (Gee 2007) are the ones that, in my experience, seem to be snatched up most often by the guys. Girls tend to pick up *Dead Is the New Black* (Perez 2008), *The Adoration of Jenna Fox* (Pearson 2008), *The Earth, My Butt, and Other Big Round Things* (Mackler 2003), *North of Beautiful* (Headley 2009), *Ghostgirl* (Hurley 2008), and *Love Me Tender* (Couloumbis 2008). If you add in the covers of all of these books, the gender gap is even more pronounced. When I was serving on the Quick Picks Committee, we joked about the "pink books." That became our not-so-covert term for a book that would appeal to girls more than boys.

Of course, covers and titles are not the only factors that play into which books appeal to boys or girls more. There are certain facets of books that tend to highlight the distinction between the sexes. Boys prefer to read books with male main characters; similarly, girls prefer to read books with female main characters. This dichotomy speaks volumes. It is one reason why the practice of having the entire class read one novel or book in common has inherent problems and why alternatives such as literature circles better meet the needs of a diverse group of readers. Offering one book, even one with a male main character, will appeal to some but not all students in a typical classroom. Though many girls will read a book with male main characters, why do we expect them to read books that may be better suited to boys? Why not offer two books, one with male main characters and one with female main characters?

Of course, a preference for main characters of one sex or the other is not the only gender difference in reading. Boys tend to prefer certain genres and subgenres. At a recent conference on tween and teen readers, both Bruce Hale and Jon Scieszka, two authors who resonate with male readers, commented on the types of books they preferred to read and that they still see attracting male readers. Humor is an important element, they assert. So is adventure. Fantasy as a genre often appeals more to the guys (though Harry Potter might have put an end to that division once and for all). And don't forget nonfiction. Last year, I was invited to speak to all the boys in a high school in south Texas. Which book did they snatch immediately? *Bat Boy Lives* (Perel and the editors of the *Weekly World News* 2005), a collection of headlines and stories from the *Weekly World News*, a tabloid that features stories about aliens, Elvis sightings, and celebrity high jinks. The librarian ordered ten copies of each book shared with the guys and reported that this one book never seemed to get back on the shelf. One teen would bring it in with a friend in tow who wanted to check it out. The book, all ten copies, stayed in circulation all year long.

So, what appeals to girls? Often female readers prefer internal character development as opposed to external descriptions of the characters. They prefer to know how their characters feel and respond to others. They prefer an intimate setting. They prefer a small cast of characters (shades of Jessica and Elizabeth in the Sweet Valley High series) and a short time span in which the story takes place. So, in a book such as *Bridge to Terabithia* (Paterson 2007), female readers will care more about how Jesse and Leslie feel than how they look. They will enjoy the familiar settings of the classroom, the living room, and the neighborhood where Jesse and Leslie live, whereas boys might focus more on the imaginative kingdom Jesse creates with Leslie.

What is important here is that the line between what female and male readers want in books is not made of concrete. There are plenty of books that have both male and female appeal. Certainly the adventures of Harry Potter demonstrated that one book can appeal to male and female, old and young, struggling and able readers. However, it is still essential to understand that there are few books that will appeal across the board to the range of readers in our classrooms. And remember, knowing about the gender differences and offering alternatives that will appeal to both male and female readers is essential, particularly in a profession that is largely female. Since many of us who work with tweens and teens are female, it means that we know the characteristics of books that will appeal to girls. We were once girls, after all. It is up to us to be equally sensitive to what the boys are looking for in a good book, too.

A final thought about gender: just because boys and girls want different things in books does not mean that we do not occasionally suggest that boys read books with a strong female protagonist or that girls read a book that is more appealing to boys; these differences between the genders are generalizations only. Differences do exist, but they do not need to polarize readers. Instead, take this information and apply it to your own classroom as needed.

School Variables

The variables within the school setting are perhaps the easiest for us to control. We often speak of creating an environment for reading, a *reading climate*. What elements are crucial in developing an atmosphere in the classroom and in the school that will aid in motivating students?

I visit quite a few schools each year. Generally, I can assess the reading environment as I walk down the hallways, visiting classrooms and the school library. Classroom libraries, the school library, and administrative support go a long way in establishing an environment that sends an often unspoken but essential message: reading is valued here. Classroom libraries signal that reading is valued sufficiently so that funds are provided for books in each and every classroom. School libraries, if adequately funded and staffed by certified personnel, also indicate a school that places value on books and reading. Administrative support is essential, too. Supervisors who understand the importance of books and reading provide not only funding but other support as well. Let's delve a little deeper into each of these components of the reading environment.

CLASSROOM LIBRARIES

Books and a comfortable place to read are two key components of a classroom that invites readers. Giles (2005) surveyed students in grades 7–12 for her doctoral dissertation to determine which activities they found motivating. One of the top responses from the students dealt with having access to books in the classroom. Classroom libraries eliminate potential barriers to student engagement. Did the student fail to bring a book to read to class? No worries: there are plenty of books on the shelves from which to select. What about the student who finishes a book before reading time is over? Again, shelves of books are near at hand. There is no need to send students to their lockers or the library; books surround them.

Understanding that students prefer to read in a more relaxed position than sitting at a desk is, to me, just common sense. I rarely sit upright at a desk and read. The closest I come to this is airplane reading. Even then, if the seat reclines, I do tend to lean back and curl up as much as the cramped space permits. Students are no exception. They, too, prefer to find a comfortable position in which to read. I hunted for beanbag chairs at garage sales to add to my classroom collection. They are easy to clean and to keep clean (pillows can house too many critters for classroom use), and students simply love to squish them into comfortable shapes for lounging on the floor and reading. I never had a problem with students being tardy to my classes, probably because each class began with time set aside for silent reading. They sprawled on the floor and under tables. Beanbags were first come, first served, so students needed to hightail it to class to claim one.

A good classroom library is more than simply a collection of books set up on shelves or in bins or boxes. Books selected for the classroom library should be subject to some critical analysis. Read more about that analysis in Chapter 4.

Classroom libraries, the school library, and administrative support go a long way in establishing an environment that sends an often unspoken but essential message: reading is valued here.

SCHOOL LIBRARY

In addition to having access to books in their own classrooms, many students in the Giles study responded that they enjoyed regular visits to the school library. Going to the library to check out books to read is something that middle and high school students find motivating. However, for some students, the library can be overwhelming. Thousands of books might be frightening to someone who is not already an avid reader. Mary Burkey, librarian extraordinaire, often uses library tables to display books for those overwhelmed by the crowded shelves. She places books with terrific covers and titles (remember those reluctant reader criteria), books both new and old, on tables in a free-form sort of display. Students who are shelf shocked can go directly to this narrowed selection to find a good book. Kylene Beers describes a "good book box," which operates in much the same way. Variations abound. My friend Lois Buckman has carts arranged around the library with signs attached. Sometimes the carts contain books from the state reading lists; sometimes the cart is for a specific class coming to the library to work on a project. Occasionally, there is a cart of new books or one containing this month's featured genre. In April, Lois features novels in verse since April is National Poetry Month. Students enjoy visiting Mary's and Lois' libraries because these women have made it simpler to find good books to read.

ADMINISTRATIVE SUPPORT

Having the support of the school administration can make a huge difference in developing a climate of reading within the school. Support can take different forms, but certainly monetary support is essential. Funds for purchasing books for classroom and school libraries, book sets, author visits, and other literacy-related activities are often difficult to come by in these times of shrinking budgets. The payoff is immense, though, and enlightened administrators know that access to books and authors helps improve not only attitudes toward books and reading but frequently test scores as well.

> **Having the support of the school administration can make a huge difference in developing a climate of reading within the school.**

Administrators can also offer support of another kind—time to read within the school day. This time, even if only ten to fifteen minutes, can be invaluable. Students are a captive audience during the school day. *We* control the environment, and we know that providing reading time can help develop some good reading habits. Time for sustained silent reading daily sends students an unspoken message: reading is an essential part of education, so important that we take time daily for its practice.

Years ago, when I was teaching in an open concept school, I began doing silent reading after lunchtime. Students came to my classroom, found those wonderful beanbags, and sprawled out on the floor to read. Since there were no walls between our students and students from other seventh-grade teams, classes on either side of my "room" could see my students, and it was not long before they began to exert pressure on the social studies and math teachers to let them do the same. The silent reading idea spread, and eventually, time was set aside daily for the entire school to participate in reading for fifteen minutes a day. This type of support is also important if the school is to ensure a positive reading environment for its students. In *The SSR Handbook*, Pilgreen (2000) discusses how to set up a sustained silent reading program in the classroom. Another valuable resource for SSR is Jodi Marshall's *Are They Really Reading?* (2002).

* * *

Motivating readers is no simple task. What might motivate one student does not necessarily motivate another. A book that excites one class might fail miserably with another. Occasionally, I see someone refer to a book as perfect for every reader. In reality, there is not one book that will appeal, at least equally, to all our students. Instead, knowing all the factors to take into consideration is essential. In the following chapter, we'll explore taking motivated readers to the next level: lifetime readers.

Creating Lifelong Readers

chapter
4

In Chapter 3, I discussed student and school variables that play roles in encouraging and supporting readers. We have a sense of what kids want to read, we've allotted time and guidance, and we have the support of other teachers, librarians, and administrators. So, where do we go from here? What can teachers and librarians do to provide students the experiences they need? I have found that the key elements are building a classroom library, reading aloud, booktalking, and being the go-to person when it comes to books. Here are some guidelines for implementing these factors.

Building a Classroom Library

A classroom library is not merely a collection of books, nor is it a kit you can purchase already constructed. Instead, a classroom library is built one book at a time *by you* to fit the individual needs and interests of your students. Here are some guiding questions to consider as you begin to build your own classroom library or add to the collection you already possess.

Is this a book that will appeal to the students in your classes? Each class and each year is different. Sometimes books need to be removed and new ones added. Books can be as faddish as tastes in clothing and music: Teenage Mutant Ninja Turtle books give way to Choose Your Own Adventure, and those give way to Animorphs, which give way to A Series of Unfortunate Events and Artemis Fowl and so on. Some books will remain year after year; others can be given out as rewards to students at the end of the school year. One place to begin to look for the books that appeal to tweens and teens is the "Teens Top Ten" list from YALSA. Each year, teens are invited to vote for their favorite books from a preselected list (where teens get to nominate their favorites). Here is the "Teens Top Ten" from 2008. More than eight thousand teens voted these ten books as their favorites from the previous year.

1. *Eclipse*, by Stephenie Meyer (2008b)
2. *Harry Potter and the Deathly Hallows*, by J. K. Rowling (2007)
3. *Diary of a Wimpy Kid*, by Jeff Kinney (2007)
4. *Vampire Academy*, by Richelle Mead (2007)
5. *Maximum Ride: Saving the World and Other Extreme Sports*, by James Patterson (2007)
6. *City of Bones*, by Cassandra Clare (2007)
7. *The Sweet Far Thing*, by Libba Bray (2007)
8. *Extras*, by Scott Westerfeld (2007)
9. *Before I Die*, by Jenny Downham (2007)
10. *Twisted*, by Laurie Halse Anderson (2007)

This list includes some books that will appeal more to boys (*Diary of a Wimpy Kid*) and some that will attract girls (*Before I Die*). They range from contemporary fiction (*Twisted*) to fantasy (*Maximum Ride*), with a preponderance of books about vampires (*Eclipse, City of Bones, Vampire Academy*). Some are part of a series of books (*Harry Potter and the Deathly Hallows, Extras, Sweet Far Thing, Eclipse*), though most of them stand alone and can be read as individual titles.

Is the book appropriate for your students? Certainly we want to ensure that the books we offer our students are in line with their development. Intellectual, moral, emotional, and social development all play roles in how books meet the needs of readers. Students who try to read books that require reasoning beyond their development may often fail to connect. For instance, if a student is still a fairly concrete learner, a book that deals with abstractions may be frustrating or confusing. Likewise,

Certainly we want to ensure that the books we offer our students are in line with their development.

students who still operate at a reward-or-punishment level of moral development may not be able to comprehend how someone can act selflessly in defense of another person. I think this is why many of the classics fail to connect with our students. Since they were written for an adult audience (Hawthorne never saw *The Scarlet Letter* as a novel for teens, I am certain), the themes presented are often developmentally inappropriate for younger readers.

Look at the "Teens Top Ten" list again. Some of the titles are more appropriate for tweens (*Diary of a Wimpy Kid*) and some are more developmentally appropriate for older teens (*Twisted*). Knowing where your students are developmentally will assist you in choosing books for your classroom collection.

Does the book possess some of the qualities that would attract less-than-avid readers? Think back to the earlier discussion in Chapter 3 about titles, covers, opening paragraphs, and the factors that motivate students to pick up books on their own. While not all books need to meet these indicators, a good classroom collection should reflect what we already know about attracting readers to books.

Are there books to appeal to a wide range of readers? Even within one classroom, there will be a range of reading abilities, interests, and preferences. Make certain there are graphic novels, comics, manga, novels in verse, pop-ups, sophisticated books, and picture books. The range also needs to encompass both fiction and nonfiction and have representation across different genres.

Do you have enough boy books? I try to make sure that I have an equal number of books for boys and for girls. This is not always an easy task. However, there are resources out there for assistance. Jon Scieszka's brainchild, www.guysread.com/, offers plenty of titles to get started. Many of the titles on the "Quick Picks for Reluctant Readers" lists (access them through the YALSA website at www.ala.org/yalsa/) are boy friendly. Hang out and listen to the conversations boys have with one another for some idea of topics that interest them. That is also a way to develop your nonfiction selections. And, of course, asking boys about what they want in books is always a good idea. Marjie Podzielinski, a wonderful librarian who works with tweens, draws names each month and takes the winners to the bookstore with the monies she has collected from overdue- and lost-book fines. Those students have the chance to buy books to add to her library collection. Their names are placed inside the books, and the books are processed and made part of the school's library. How powerful is this simple idea for making certain that students have a voice in what is added to the shelves!

How are your books arranged? There is no one way to arrange the books in your classroom library. However, there does need to be some organized arrangement so that you and your students can find the books readily. I used to arrange most of mine by genre and then alphabetically by author within each genre. I have seen bins of books collected by theme, and I think there is merit to that concept, too. Involving students in some of this decision making is also a positive step. Remember that these students are consummate shoppers and want to be able to locate what they want quickly. In fact, they might be able to suggest a simple system. There is also no reason why different systems of organization can't be utilized from year to year. What is paramount is that we know how to find the books instantly and can then show students how to do the same on their own.

Have you read all the books in the collection? There is some disagreement about this issue among educators. I believe that we need to know all the titles we have on the shelves in our classroom. After all, I would never ask my graduate students to read a book I do not know well. How can we have a conversation with students if we do not know the content of the books? If we know what is there, we should have no trouble at all defending a book should someone raise an objection. Just because a book has won an award or is on a list from a professional organization does not make it appropriate for your students. *The Giver* (Lowry 2002), a Newbery winner, found its way into many elementary classrooms and school libraries once it had won the award, but it requires a certain level of sophistication from its readers. Similarly, some of the recipients of the Printz Award are more appropriate for high school than middle school readers. While I am not advocating that teachers shy away from problematic content (e.g., language, violence, sexuality, drugs), I do think that reading the books on our shelves make us better prepared to defend it should it be challenged.

Reading Aloud and Booktalking

Two never-fail strategies—I call them *teachniques*—are also important components of creating readers. Reading aloud and booktalking should be part of every teacher's bag of tricks, though many teachers take on their first classroom never having been introduced to them. I, for one, never had coursework that included these strategies. Reading aloud was never stressed because I was taking coursework to become a secondary teacher, and it was accepted that one reads aloud only to elementary-aged children. Booktalking was not deemed a necessary component,

> Reading aloud and booktalking should be part of every teacher's bag of tricks, though many teachers take on their first classroom never having been introduced to them.

either, as the entire literature curriculum was also proscribed for us. And then I received my first job in education.

I began teaching a self-contained eighth-grade class in December of the school year. I was the third teacher for that particular class, a class composed of African Americans, a few Hispanics, and two Caucasians. It was a small Catholic school in an impoverished neighborhood; there were few textbooks and no formal school library. I began reading aloud as a way of making certain that all the students had a common reading experience. As I began to accumulate some books for a classroom library, I came to class and talked about the books so that students could make informed choices. Years later, I learned that reading aloud and booktalking were not just effective approaches for me in my desperation but research-proven strategies for connecting readers and books.

READING ALOUD

Professional resources abound on the value of reading aloud to elementary students. However, I have found some of these quite useful for secondary students as well. Mem Fox's *Reading Magic* (2008), though intended for an audience of parents, has proven useful for many teachers who want to be able to communicate to their administration about why they read aloud to students who are expected to be able to read independently. In the simplest terms, Fox discusses why reading aloud will change the lives of our children. Jim Trelease's *Read-Aloud Handbook* (2006) also reviews the research into the effectiveness of reading aloud with children of all ages. Chapters are devoted to reading aloud in other professional books as well. I have written extensively about reading aloud in my own books *Making the Match: The Right Book for the Right Reader at the Right Time* (2003) and *Naked Reading* (2006) and in chapters I have contributed to other books, including Beers, Probst, and Rief's *Adolescent Literacy: Turning Promise into Practice* (2007). Time and again, I come to the same conclusion: Reading aloud is simple and effective. It models fluency for students; it motivates students to pick up books to read; and it develops skills in listening and reading comprehension.

Reading aloud to our students models how the book should *sound*. How do words and phrases connect in this sentence and the next one? How is that word pronounced? What role does punctuation play? Students who are learning English as a second language can profit from hearing books read aloud as it answers the preceding questions. Students who struggle with text for any number of reasons (e.g., dyslexia, poor vocabulary, lack of comprehension skills) can also profit from having a teacher who reads aloud. Quite frankly, I still love being read aloud to at my ripe old age. It is one of the reasons why audiobooks are part of my daily life, especially my commutes to and from classes on and off campus.

Reading aloud can also motivate students to select books to read. Often, I elect to read short passages from a variety of books to entice students. I call this approach to reading aloud *read and tease*, as I read only a piece of the book, just enough to whet appetites. As I read books, I search for passages that will make good candidates for this approach. I mark them with sticky notes so I can find them easily, and once I have a handful or so, I take the books into the classroom and proceed to share the passages aloud. More often than not, those books are checked out immediately and find their readers.

Think of finding books using this analogy: When you go out to buy a new car, sometimes you know exactly what you want. You want the same make and model of car you already have. It serves you well; there is no need to make a change. But occasionally, you want a new driving experience. How do you go about selecting *this* car? Generally, you visit different dealers, test-drive vehicles, and then compare their various qualities before making your final selection. Students who already know what they want and need in books require little from us. For some students, though, more guidance is necessary. Listening to passages from a variety of books is similar to taking those test drives and determining what qualities they want in their books. So reading aloud often and from a wide range of texts assists students in locating books to read on their own.

Finally, reading aloud can develop skills in listening and reading comprehension. I do not intend that reading aloud be transformed into a skill-and-drill time, but from time to time, some skills can be reinforced. Ask students to summarize the read-aloud occasionally. Have them make notes of any words that were unfamiliar or unusual. Students could pose a question at the end of the read-aloud or make a prediction. They could begin to develop an outline of the plot or craft a character sketch. Context clues, basic comprehension, and even more advanced literary analysis are possible with reading aloud. Do remember, though, that the primary purpose of reading aloud is to connect students to books. It should remain a time of enjoyment, an aesthetic experience.

BOOKTALKING

In a 2009 article in *VOYA* (*Voice of Youth Advocates*), Ruth Cox Clark reported on a two-year period in which more than one hundred educators talked about books to almost three thousand students. Students were quick to indicate their interest in booktalks and their preference for three different approaches to booktalking.

Booktalking, long the purview of librarians, is the subject of numerous books, including a series from Ruth Cox Clark and Joni Bodart complete with sample booktalks for hundreds of books. Websites contain podcasts of booktalks as well. A simple Google search will result in more than a half a million hits. Visit Nancy Keane's site (www.nancykeane.com/) for some examples of booktalks and some podcasts of her talks. Joni Bodart also provides podcasts, videos, and other examples at the Scholastic website (teacher.scholastic.com/products/tradebooks/booktalks.htm). To get you started, here are the three essential components to a successful booktalk.

Finding the Right Book

Some books do not need to be introduced personally to students. They are what I call the *move out of the way* books. Their titles and covers sell them to readers, even reluctant readers. When I am deciding which books to include in a booktalk, I am looking for those books that might not sell themselves but that should, with some guidance, find the right audience. Before Stephenie Meyer's books became a cultural phenomenon, I decided to do a booktalk about *Twilight* (2005) to a class of eighth graders. There was nothing on the cover (save the shape of the letter *l* noticed only by those who look carefully) to indicate this was a book about a teenage girl falling in love with a vampire. By now, of course, millions of readers know and love the books about Bella and Edward. And since vampires are currently a hot subject, I would include some other stories about vampires that might not have appeared on the radar of my audience.

Knowing the importance and appeal of humor, I do try to include funny books in a booktalk. The Jack books, largely autobiographical stories of the life of author Jack Gantos, are some of my favorites. *Jack on the Tracks* (1999), *Jack's Black Book* (2005), and *Jack's New Power* (1997) are all wonderfully humorous and easy to talk about with students. Sometimes I read a passage (there is a great scene about a tapeworm in one book, one about a cockroach in another). Sometimes I opt simply to tell what about the book appealed to me (and that I think will appeal to my audience). Jon Scieszka's *Knucklehead* (2008) is largely autobiographical, too, and talks about growing up in a family of six boys. I might ask who has brothers and sisters. Who is the oldest in his or her family? The youngest? The middle child? These are all touch points that will connect readers to this book.

In general, a book that I will talk about is a book that elicited some strong response from me. It might have made me laugh or cry. It might have made me angry, so angry I threw the book across the room. Or it might have made me wince in familiarity when something experienced by one of the characters struck a personal chord. What this means is that the books you might elect to include in a booktalk could be quite different from the ones I would select. Booktalking is rather idiosyncratic. You might, then, consider asking a colleague to talk about books with you. I have a handful of colleagues with whom I have done booktalks. It never fails that I find the books they talk about so interesting that I seek out the unfamiliar ones and read them. Your school librarian is the best place to begin if you want to include a colleague. He or she is most likely just waiting for the chance to be asked to talk about books to your students. Bonus: a school librarian can help you locate those just-right books, too.

Finding the Right Way to Tell Students About the Book

The point of the booktalk is to sell the book. You want to tell just enough about the book to whet the appetite of the reader. Tell too much and you have ruined the book (remember when someone told you the secret to *The Sixth Sense*?). Tell too little and you won't generate enough excitement. Some people opt to become one of the characters from the novel and speak about the book as if it were her personal story. Reading aloud a short passage from early on in the story is another approach to beginning a booktalk. Follow up the read-aloud passage by talking about the conflict or some exciting incident or the setting (this works well with futuristic novels and historical fiction or science fiction set in another time or place).

Once you are comfortable with booktalking, try some other variations. One of my favorite formats is to say one or two sentences about a book and then move on to the next. Quick and dirty booktalks can work with certain types of books. Recently, a colleague of mine and I created a podcast of booktalks titled *Life Sucks*. Here is a snapshot of this approach to booktalking.

> Life sucks when you are a cheerleader and have to have your leg amputated (*Izzy, Willy-Nilly*, by Cynthia Voigt [2005]).
>
> Life sucks when you choke to death on a gummy bear on the first day of a new school year (*Ghostgirl*, by Tonya Hurley [2008]).
>
> Life sucks when you discover the friend you made online is actually a predator (*Exposed*, by Susan Vaught [2008]).
>
> Life sucks when all your friends get the cool fairies and all yours is good for is finding good parking spots (*How to Ditch Your Fairy*, by Justine Larbalestier [2008]).

For the podcast, we located the sound effect of a baby sucking on a bottle and placed it in the background of the booktalks. We added some other titles specifically about blood suckers (vampires, of course) and then posted the podcast for our students.

The best tip I can provide here is to always read with sticky notes in hand. I mark potential passages for reading aloud and jot down notes about what I want to say about the books as I read them. One of my colleagues writes out her booktalks and then practices them so she can talk about books without her notes. Some prefer to place a sticky note on the back of the book with the names of the main characters or other things they wish to include. I tend to prefer to do booktalks off the cuff. However, if you are just starting out, notes and drafts and other techniques will be valuable and make you feel more comfortable talking about books. After a while, this will be so natural that you can pick up a book you have just read and talk about it.

Finding a Way to Connect One Book to Another and Another

It is not enough, generally speaking, to talk about only one book. Thus, there is a need for segues that move you from one book to the next and so on. Don't constantly rely on the phrase *the next book*. Connecting one book to another and another and another is important, and not just for booktalking. Making connections between and among books is something that lifelong readers do naturally—not so for most middle and high school students. So, if we demonstrate those connections to them in this concrete manner, we are not only providing an interesting booktalk but also showing students how books can connect in a variety of different ways: character, theme, setting, conflict, and the like.

Becoming the Go-To Book Person

Many years ago, I began to offer my services as a booktalker to school libraries in the greater Houston area. When I left the middle school classroom for the university, I missed the interaction with tweens and teens. I wanted to keep in touch with the students who had been instrumental in my education on the job. One day, I received a phone call from a former library science student who was now the librarian at the intermediate school where my oldest granddaughter, Cali, was then in fifth grade. The librarian and I chatted for a while and she asked if I would like to come and do some booktalks for Cali's class when it came to the library. How could I refuse? When I arrived on the agreed upon day, I found myself talking to the entire school population in the cafeteria. Talk about an intimidating audience. I talked about a dozen or so books, thanked the librarian, and headed home.

I felt the booktalks had gone well, and after I returned home that afternoon, I fixed dinner and went about the usual routine for the evening. The phone rang shortly after bath time. When I answered, the voice at the other end asked if I was the person who had been talking to the students at Cali's school that day. This was a parent of one of the fifth graders who had been in the audience. I braced myself for a complaint about one of the books, since I had talked about mysteries, humorous books, and nonfiction for a wide range of readers. However, as it turns out, this parent called to thank me for turning her son onto some books she had been trying (unsuccessfully) to get him to read. She was a school librarian in a neighboring district. What had I done that had made a difference to this student? I was the outsider who came into the school and made students laugh, and wince, and gasp. I knew the good books, and I managed to let students know which books they might enjoy as well.

Kylene Beers often calls me the "book woman." It is a label I love as it succinctly describes my passion in life. You should aspire to be known as the book person in your classroom and in your school. Be the one who knows the good books and shares them through reading aloud and book-talking. Be the person who has those good books in the classroom and who knows how to help students find them in the school library as well. Be the go-to teacher who knows good books for boys and for reluctant readers, for girls and for troubled teens. Be the person who can bring students into the reading club.

You should aspire to be known as the book person in your classroom and in your school.

Building Reading Ladders

chapter

5

In the opening chapters of this book, we considered how to motivate students to read. Our job, though, is only half done. Once we connect students to books, we cannot abandon them. We need to provide them with some guidance to help them continue to develop as readers. Why is this so important?

I had a childhood friend who would eat only selected items: tomato soup, grilled cheese sandwiches, and French fries. The reason that this friend had such limited tastes is that her parents never made it an issue. She was always free to select what she wanted to eat. In childhood, this is a cute eccentricity. In the adult world, this can be rather limiting. Try to host a dinner party that way! Add to this dilemma the fact that this limited menu is not the healthiest, and it is easy to see why we must expose youngsters to other foods. And so it goes with books and reading. While there is absolutely nothing wrong with developing strong preferences in books at any age, it is imperative that we open students to the entire world of books.

My own world of books was severely limited at one point. As an English education major, I took dozens of classes in literature: Chaucer, Shakespeare, Hemingway, and other classic authors were part of my studies. What was lacking? Nonfiction. I had plenty of coursework with poetry, drama, short stories, and novels. However, my exposure to nonfiction was limited to an occasional essay by Thoreau. Nonfiction, it seemed to me, was the domain of other content areas.

As I began to work with middle school students, I noticed another gap in my own literary education: science fiction and fantasy. Science fiction and fantasy were the top picks among many of my middle school boys, but I had read very little of it, as had many of the teachers within my English department. Since I did not grow up with Harry Potter, fantasy, especially high fantasy with its elements of archetypes and motifs and timeless good versus evil themes, was not a genre I read much. None of the required reading in high school or college seemed to include this genre, either. I took it upon myself to slowly fill in the gaps. However, I wonder how many of our students, if left to their own devices, would or could fill in gaps? It is up to us to help them taste a wide variety of books. But beyond showing students a wide variety of genre, forms, and formats, there is another part to our task: helping them grow as readers.

Often, we read in either a horizontal or vertical movement. In horizontal reading, we read books serially. Specializing in an author's works or in the works of one series, we find comfort: Each book is quite like the one before. We know what to expect in terms of plot and character and resolution. There are few surprises. I recall fondly the hours spent solving mysteries with Nancy Drew or healing the sick with Cherry Ames or surviving some dark menace in my Gothic romance novels. I enjoyed reading series books and still do, frequently indulging in novels by Sue Grafton, Patricia Cornwell, and other adult authors.

Vertical reading seems to be the domain of secondary school reading. In vertical reading, we move ever upward. Elementary poetry, for instance, which involves humorous verses and lots of puns and other funny plays on words, gives way to classic forms and poets. We move from "ha ha ha" to haiku without much of a transition to assist our students. *The Outsiders* (Hinton 1967) gives way to *Hamlet* (Shakespeare 2003). *Memoirs of a Teenage Amnesiac* (Zevin 2007) fades into essays by Thoreau and Emerson with nary a bridge to help readers cross successfully. Vertical reading is where we lose many readers, I fear. The path is too steep and there are few guideposts along the way to assist the inexperienced climber. What I propose is more of a diagonal movement, just the situation for reading ladders.

Reading ladders take students from one level of reading to the next logical level. If students like certain types of books, certain genres,

Reading ladders take students from one level of reading to the next logical level.

or certain qualities in a book, we can help them stretch as readers by showing them books that mirror what they already like but that perhaps are a little longer, are a bit more abstract, or will challenge them more. Let me say at the outset that I am most decidedly not in favor of constantly moving students to longer and more challenging texts. As an adult, it is lovely to "read easy" from time to time. Students, too, need to occasionally plateau and linger in their comfort zone. However, when students are struggling to find that next great book, we should be able to step in and help them move along.

Eventually, students will become more adept at finding books themselves. While they are still developing, though, we need to do all we can to help them locate books that reflect their interests and preferences, books that will move them painlessly from where they are to where we would like them to be.

Getting Started

We need to start with a familiar foundation and build slowly, fitting the pieces together gradually until we have a stronger, more complex whole.

The concept of reading ladders is as simple as the concept of building with those Lincoln Logs we talked about earlier. We need to start with a familiar foundation and build slowly, fitting the pieces together gradually until we have a stronger, more complex whole. Here are some of the basics of reading ladders to help you custom build them for *your* students.

What is a reading ladder? Simply, a reading ladder is a series or set of books that are related in some way (e.g., thematically) and that demonstrate a slow, gradual development from simple to more complex. Ideally, the first rung of the reading ladder is a book that already has found a connection to the student. The second rung is a book that is almost identical to the first, thereby making it likely that the student will read it. At each successive rung, the books are still reminiscent of the ones that preceded them but are increasingly complex. Sometimes the books move from genre to genre; occasionally, the books remain within a genre. There are no hard-and-fast rules here. The intent is to move readers from their comfort zone to books that represent more diversity.

How do reading ladders work? Did you ever have a student ask you for a book "just like" the one he had finished recently? These students have found that perfect book and want more books like it but don't know how to locate them. Reading ladders provide that wonderful scaffolding that emerging lifetime readers need by helping them find other books that offer satisfying reading experiences. However, a ladder will work only if the steps are close together. Too often, we ask our students to take great leaps. Remember that example of poetry in the elementary grades? Students in those early grades delight in the humorous wordplay of X. J. Kennedy; they adore Shel Silverstein and Jack Prelutsky. They delve into collections of poems about holidays and other familiar topics, like those from Lee Bennett Hopkins. Then comes middle school poetry. Gone is the humor. In many cases, these topics are neither familiar nor important to the students. Think for a moment about the gulf that exists between poems such as "Homework," by Jack Prelutsky, which begins with the line "Homework, oh homework, I hate you. You stink" (1984, 54), and Robert Frost's "Whose woods these are, I think I know" (2001, 3), from the poem "Stopping by Woods on a Snowy Evening." This is not a case of moving from one rung to the next. This is leaping over a gaping chasm in terms of the depth of experience the reader needs to appreciate the poem fully. Reading ladders are how students can move gradually from Prelutsky to Frost.

How do I get started with reading ladders? I advise beginning with a short survey (see Figure 5.1) of students and their reading interests and preferences. A checklist that includes a variety of genres, forms, and formats can provide useful information. Other items to include might be a checklist of titles and authors, so that we can see what other reading experiences our students have had. Please note that this is not an exhaustive list. You will need to personalize it to suit the ages and interests of your students. Also, be careful not to overwhelm students with long surveys and checklists; it is better to do several shorter surveys over a few weeks. And don't forget the value of talking to your colleagues and eavesdropping on your students!

How can I make students more independent? Readers need to have many successful experiences with books before they are ready to become more independent. I think we sometimes expect students to be independent too soon. In the era of NCLB, for instance, reading aloud has been abandoned after third grade because students are expected to be independent readers. In that context, *independence* seems to equate with *solitary*, but reading is not always a solitary experience. Communities of readers, people who can discuss books and reading, remain important to us long after we are graduated. So, classrooms should be communities where we support one another as developing readers. If we are successful, we can teach our students to assist one another in locating books to read, allowing us to step aside gradually in favor of our new student experts. Complete independence in selecting books is never the goal of reading ladders, nor should it be the goal of the reading program. Instead, our goal is to open

STUDENT SURVEY

Place a check mark in the blank before any of the following types of books you enjoy reading for pleasure. After you are done, go back and mark your top three choices by placing the numbers 1 through 3 in the blanks next to the check marks.

_____biography

_____autobiography

_____war stories

_____graphic novels

_____comic books

_____manga

_____school stories

_____fantasy

_____realistic fiction

_____how-to books

_____historical fiction

_____poetry

_____stories

_____drama (plays)

_____series books (which ones?)

_____science fiction

_____real stories

_____drawing books

Place a check mark in front of the names of the books and authors you know from the following list. If you have read the book or books by this author and enjoyed them, place a plus sign (+) after the title or author's name.

_____*Charlotte's Web* (White 2006)

_____Gary Paulsen

_____Baby-Sitter's Club series

_____Harry Potter books

_____*The True Story of the 3 Little Pigs* (Scieszka 1999)

_____Gossip Girls series

_____Jon Scieszka

_____Chris Crutcher

_____*Where the Red Fern Grows* (Rawls 2000)

_____Chronicles of Narnia

_____Shel Silverstein

_____Brian Selznick

_____*The Watsons Go to Birmingham—1963* (Curtis 1995)

_____Sammy Keyes mysteries

_____*Guinness World Records* (Guinness World Records Limited 2009)

_____Russell Freedman

_____*Holes* (Sachar 2008)

_____Joey Pigza books

_____Lemony Snicket books

_____*The Giver* (Lowry 2002)

_____Will Hobbs

_____The Clique series

_____Stephenie Meyer

_____Jack Gantos

_____*Bridge to Terabithia* (Paterson 2007)

_____Magic Tree House books

_____Jack Prelutsky

_____Jacqueline Woodson

_____Lee J. Ames

_____Chet Gecko mysteries

_____Laurence Pringle

_____Diane Stanley

Figure 5.1 *Student Survey*

the world of books to our students and to share with them how we, as adults, find the good books. I, for one, always want to be a resource for my students. I want them to ask me about good books, about what to read next. I still rely on recommendations of books from colleagues and from reviews and listservs. Yes, I can select books on my own, books that meet my tastes and interests. However, I might well miss out on many terrific books if I were totally independent in my selections.

How many steps should there be on a typical reading ladder? If only education were that simple, right? The answer to this question depends on where the student begins and where we would like her to proceed. Another factor that plays a role here includes the genre, form, and format of the book with which we begin. Student variables might also come into play. Sometimes a reading ladder looks more like a step stool. Other times, the reading ladder might appear to be more of the extension sort of ladder that can grow and reach as far as need be.

Creating a Reading Ladder

There are some rules, so to speak, as we prepare to create these first reading ladders. The books that will occupy the bottom and the top rungs are important determinations. The bottom rung should always be a book that students will read without much prodding. The top rung is, ideally, the one we believe students can achieve at the top of the ladder. Begin with small reading ladders that move students just a degree or two. As you develop more reading ladders, you can extend them to cover the course of a grading period or a semester or an academic year. Wouldn't it be lovely if we met with our counterparts in lower and upper grades and worked on reading ladders that followed students from one level to another? For now, let's start small.

Since mystery is one genre that is enjoyed equally by male and female readers, why not begin with this genre for our first reading ladder? Figures 5.2a and 5.2b are visual representations of variations on the Whodunit ladder. The bottom rung should be a book accessible for all our readers in one class or grade. Jay Bennett's *Executioner* (1982) might be one place to begin construction. While this book has a YA interest level, the reading level is about fourth grade. It is a quick read and perfect for reluctant readers with its short chapters often ending with cliffhangers. If needed, we could even reach a bit lower with our bottom rung and begin with the popular mysteries in intermediate grades, including the funny Chet Gecko mysteries by Bruce Hale (titles include *Murder, My Tweet* [1994] and *The Malted Falcon*

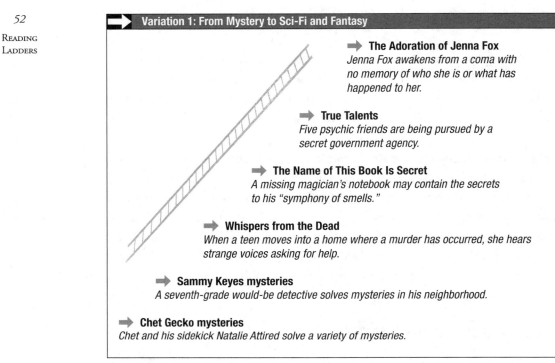

Variation 1: From Mystery to Sci-Fi and Fantasy

The Adoration of Jenna Fox
Jenna Fox awakens from a coma with no memory of who she is or what has happened to her.

True Talents
Five psychic friends are being pursued by a secret government agency.

The Name of This Book Is Secret
A missing magician's notebook may contain the secrets to his "symphony of smells."

Whispers from the Dead
When a teen moves into a home where a murder has occurred, she hears strange voices asking for help.

Sammy Keyes mysteries
A seventh-grade would-be detective solves mysteries in his neighborhood.

Chet Gecko mysteries
Chet and his sidekick Natalie Attired solve a variety of mysteries.

Figure 5.2a *Variations on the Whodunit Ladder*

[2003]) and the Sammy Keyes series by Wendelin Van Draanen (e.g., *Sammy Keyes and the Hotel Thief* [1998]).

Now we should determine the top rung of the ladder. Perhaps a short story by Sir Arthur Conan Doyle would suit. Or we might wish students to reach the top rung with another (though more complex) YA mystery, such as *The Corps of the Bare-Boned Plane*, by Polly Horvath (2007), or *The London Eye Mystery*, by Siobhan Dowd (2008). We could even mix genres a bit and have the topmost rung be a mystery with a bit of a science fiction flair, such as *The Adoration of Jenna Fox*, by Mary Pearson (2008).

Once we have set the top and bottom rungs, it is time to fill in the intervening rungs. Try some of these resources for locating mysteries for your ladder:

- Poe Award finalists for best juvenile mystery. Each year, the Mystery Writers of America bestows honors on mystery books for adults and for young readers. The group's website, www.mysterywriters.org/, lists current winners as well as past nominees and winners.

- Jeanette Larson's *Bringing Mysteries Alive for Children and Young Adults* (2004).

- *Genreflecting*, by Diana Herald (2006).

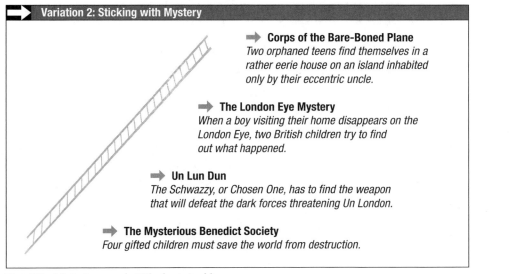

Variation 2: Sticking with Mystery

Corps of the Bare-Boned Plane
Two orphaned teens find themselves in a rather eerie house on an island inhabited only by their eccentric uncle.

The London Eye Mystery
When a boy visiting their home disappears on the London Eye, two British children try to find out what happened.

Un Lun Dun
The Schwazzy, or Chosen One, has to find the weapon that will defeat the dark forces threatening Un London.

The Mysterious Benedict Society
Four gifted children must save the world from destruction.

Figure 5.2b *Variations on the Whodunit Ladder*

- Amazon (www.amazon.com/), Barnes and Noble (www.barnesandnoble.com/), Borders (www.borders.com/), and other retail websites offer an advanced search option.

- Titlewave, a resource from the book jobber Follett (www.titlewave.com/), is another source for titles.

- Your colleagues! Nothing beats wide reading on the part of educators for building the ladders that will be most effective with students.

The bottom two rungs of the ladder in Figure 5.2a are mysteries series. Chet Gecko is a great series for younger readers, full of wonderful wordplay, as evidenced in all the hilarious puns (Natalie Attired). Sammy Keyes is a middle school student who is a rightful heir to Nancy Drew and the Hardy Boys, though with more humor. Having two series on the bottom rungs will permit less skilled readers the opportunity to pause on a step and read horizontally until they are comfortable enough to continue up the ladder. By the third step, it is possible that some readers will have finished dozens of books.

Next they will meet the grande dame of mysteries for young adults: Joan Lowery Nixon (1991), four-time winner of the Edgar Allan Poe Award for best juvenile mystery. Again, readers can pause here to read more books by Nixon until they are ready to continue to the next rung. Synesthesia plays a role in the next unlikely mystery, by Pseudonymous Bosch (1997), and you might have to point out that the author's pen name is a play on words as well. *True Talents* (Lubar 2007) and *The*

Adoration of Jenna Fox (Pearson 2008) take the mystery to a new level and bring in another genre as well.

Here, the top rung is a mystery with a science fiction premise. Therefore, the book that immediately precedes it on the ladder should also have elements of science fiction or fantasy. As a matter of fact, all of these mysteries contain elements of fantasy or science fiction. If students are still climbing this reading ladder willingly, we can now connect them to another genre and continue the climb, this time through various selections that are more fantastic than mysterious. If students resist, then we can offer them a second possibility, shown in Figure 5.2b.

In this ladder, the element of fantasy is much lighter, present mostly in *Un Lun Dun*, by China Miéville (2008). On the bottom rung of the ladder is *The Mysterious Benedict Society* (Stewart 2007). Here is a marvelous book that might be overlooked because the title and cover do little to suggest what is central to the story inside, a possibility I raised in Chapter 3, where I talked about important variables when students are selecting books. In this story, four children, each with unique gifts, answer an ad in the paper looking for children open to special opportunities. Reynie, Sticky, Kate, and Constance all are sent to the Learning Institute for the Very Enlightened to stop a madman from taking over the world. There are shades of *1984* and other classic novels running through this book. For students who appreciate the exploits of the four children, there is already a sequel that will permit them to linger a while longer on this bottom rung.

Zanna and her friend Deeba must combat highly unusual foes in *Un Lun Dun*, a novel that examines the nature of good and evil. The characters are a bit older in this novel, though the age of the main characters should not make much of a difference with these books for tweens. What connects this book with *The Mysterious Benedict Society* is the fact that the characters possess some special talents, even though they may not be aware of the nature of these talents.

The main character in *The London Eye Mystery* (Dowd 2008) is also different; Ted is autistic. As such, he is possibly the least likely person to solve a missing person's case. And yet his decidedly different way of viewing the world, colored by his autism, is exactly what makes him valuable in this mystery, despite the fact that he can sometimes drive his sister Kat up the wall.

Finally, in *The Corps of the Bare-Boned Plane* (Horvath 2007), teen cousins Meline and Jocelyn live with their strangely disengaged uncle, a butler, and a cook. Their adventures, when the rest of the household is sleeping, uncover clues about a mystery from the family's past. Students who find the eccentric and quirky world of Horvath fascinating can, of course, read more of her books, including *My One Hun-*

dred Adventures (2008), *The Canning Season* (2005), and *Everything on a Waffle* (2001). An additional natural step on this ladder could be a Dickens novel, with its strange and quirky characters, or perhaps some nonfiction that would acquaint the reader with the weird lives of Edgar Allan Poe or Hans Christian Andersen. But why stop here? Reading ladders can take off in many different directions at any given step on the ladder if you wish.

For instance, as you read the 2008 Newbery medal winner *Good Masters! Sweet Ladies!* by Laura Amy Schlitz (2007), you may see connections with other titles about medieval times, villages, and people. Imagine how this ladder might be welcome in a world history class as well. This same book might lead to a reading ladder filled with titles that lend themselves to readers theatre productions. Another possibility is to build a reading ladder of novels in verse. This format can sometimes pave the way for stepping easily into poetry.

Crossing Genre Boundaries

Content area connections are also invaluable. Newbery Honor winner *Elijah of Buxton*, by Christopher Paul Curtis (2007a), contains references to the Underground Railroad. Books that include information or references to the Underground Railroad abound in children's and YA literature. A bit more broadly, we can also connect Curtis' book to works that are set during the civil rights movement, such as *The Watsons Go to Birmingham—1963*, also by Christopher Paul Curtis (1995), *A Thousand Never Evers*, by Shana Burg (2008), and *Mississippi Trial, 1955* (2002) and *Getting Away with Murder* (2003), both by Chris Crowe. Heading in a different direction, we could create a reading ladder of humorous books with *Elijah* as well. Figures 5.3 and 5.4 demonstrate reading ladders that feature novels in verse and humor respectively. Each ladder branches off from *Elijah of Buxton* and heads in a new direction.

NOVELS IN VERSE

Novels in verse tend to be popular with readers. For some, it is because there is less text "crowding" the page, as one reluctant thirteen-year-old informed me. Additionally, it is possible in many of the novels in verse to read a chapter in one sitting because chapters are short. Let's capitalize on this interest and build a reading ladder using novels in verse (see Figure 5.3).

This reading ladder of novels in verse spans several grade levels. We can begin with Sharon Creech's *Love That Dog* (2001) and *Hate That Cat* (2008) with

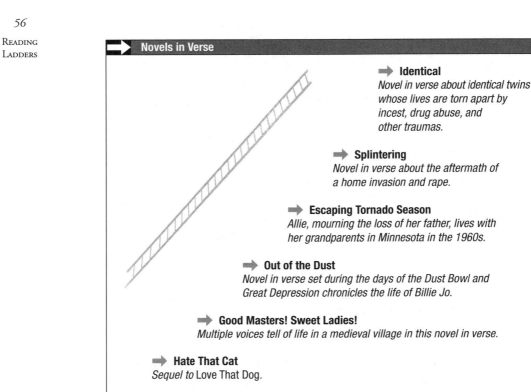

Novels in Verse

➡ **Identical**
*Novel in verse about identical twins
whose lives are torn apart by
incest, drug abuse, and
other traumas.*

➡ **Splintering**
*Novel in verse about the aftermath of
a home invasion and rape.*

➡ **Escaping Tornado Season**
*Allie, mourning the loss of her father, lives with
her grandparents in Minnesota in the 1960s.*

➡ **Out of the Dust**
*Novel in verse set during the days of the Dust Bowl and
Great Depression chronicles the life of Billie Jo.*

➡ **Good Masters! Sweet Ladies!**
Multiple voices tell of life in a medieval village in this novel in verse.

➡ **Hate That Cat**
Sequel to Love That Dog.

➡ **Love That Dog**
Jack hates poetry, but a year with Ms. Stretchberry just might change that attitude.

Figure 5.3 *Novels in Verse*

students in fifth and sixth grades. Even male readers will appreciate these two books about Jack, a student in Miss Stretchberry's class, who dislikes poetry.

The next step on this ladder is the 2008 Newbery Medal winner *Good Masters! Sweet Ladies!* (Schlitz 2007). It is perfect for presenting to the class in a readers theatre format, with students taking on the different voices and characters. Again, there is appeal to male as well as female readers in fifth and sixth grades. When we move to the next step on this ladder, however (*Out of the Dust*, by Karen Hesse [1997]), our focus is more sharply on the female readers who appreciate the format of the novel in verse.

The Newbery winner *Out of the Dust* is set in the Dust Bowl days (notice we are keeping a historical connection on this and the next step). This book will appeal more to seventh- and eighth-grade readers, as will *Escaping Tornado Season* (Williams 2004), set in the 1960s. The final two books on the ladder, *Splintering* (Corrigan 2004) and *Identical* (Hopkins 2008), deal with intense topics, including rape, vio-

Be a Clown: Humorous Reading Ladder

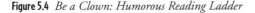

➡️ **Skulduggery Pleasant**
Skulduggery is a skeleton and private detective who comes to the aid of Stephanie when she inherits her uncle's estate.

➡️ **The Willoughbys**
The four Willoughby children long to be orphans in this parody of eighteenth-century novels about poor children.

➡️ **Millions**
When he discovers a bank bag filled with currency, Damien Cunningham and his brother try to spend as much as possible quickly.

➡️ **Elijah of Buxton**
Elijah is the first child born free in Ontario's Buxton Settlement, a refuge for escaped slaves.

➡️ **Regarding the Bathroom: A Privy to the Past**
This fictional story of a principal wanting to remodel his school's bathrooms take readers back to the beginning of indoor plumbing and headlong into a mystery as well.

➡️ **Knucklehead**
Growing up as part of a large family of boys has its ups and downs in this autobiographical story by Jon Scieszka.

➡️ **Fowl Language**
Nate and Lisa, ten-year-old twins, discover the magical ability of a rubber chicken to grant wishes.

➡️ **The Magic Pickle**
Good and bad vegetables battle in this funny graphic novel.

Figure 5.4 *Be a Clown: Humorous Reading Ladder*

lence, dependency, and incest. They are more appropriate for high school readers. By the top rung, we have left the realm of historical content behind.

The Novels in Verse ladder could easily be altered. We could use *Out of the Dust* as our bottom rung and construct a reading ladder of books dealing with the Dust Bowl (a historical period) or a ladder with a theme of dealing with adversity. Other connections with the same bottom-rung selection could include books with main characters who are musicians (involve your music department in this ladder) or, more broadly, books that connect to the arts, both visual and performing. *Out of the Dust* might also be the bottom rung for a ladder of books by Karen Hesse. The top rung in this scenario might be Hesse's other novel in verse, *Witness* (2001), with other titles such as *The Music of the Dolphins* (1998) and *Phoenix Rising* (1995) in between. These two novels could lead readers into a ladder with a science fiction emphasis, too. The possibilities are endless. Reading ladders, then, can cross boundaries of genre (realistic fiction, historical fiction, etc.) and form (novels in verse, for instance). They can also be constructed around a specific quality of a book.

MAKE THEM LAUGH: HUMOROUS READING LADDERS

In addition to mysteries, students often indicate a preference for books that are funny. Humor is developmental. Therefore, selecting books for each rung of the ladder means knowing whether or not your students will appreciate physical humor, humor based on character, situational humor, or even irony and satire. The ladder in Figure 5.4 begins with physical and situational humor and moves ever upward to irony and satire and more sophisticated forms of humor.

The Be a Clown ladder begins with a graphic novel, *The Magic Pickle*, by Scott Morse (2008), in which the Romaine Gladiator is defeated by Weapon Kosher and his sidekick, Jojo. We could easily substitute one of the books by Dav Pilkey in the Captain Underpants series here, too, or one of the Chet Gecko books we discussed under mysteries. Next on the ladder is D. L. Garfinkle's *Fowl Language* (2008), the first in the Supernatural Rubber Chicken series. While not a graphic novel, it has some illustrations scattered throughout that makes this step a painless one. Short chapters and loads of laughable situations make this a good choice for reluctant readers. Despite its younger audience, it does explore why someone must be careful when making a wish. A separate story line involving the mother of the twins provides some more laughs for older readers.

Knucklehead, by Jon Scieszka (2008), is subtitled *Tall Tales and Mostly True Stories of Growing Up Scieszka*. This is an autobiography of Scieszka's childhood, with photos of his family and some drawings to illuminate the stories. (We have switched from fiction to nonfiction at this point, but it should be an easy step for most readers, since it is the thread of humor that connects these books. It also give us another opportunity to head in a new direction with variations of this ladder. For instance, we could add more books that are autobiographical, such as Gary Paulsen's *Harris and Me* [2007] or *The Schernoff Discoveries* [1997] and *Oddballs*, by William Sleator [1993].)

Continuing up the humor ladder, the next step could be another book that has some components of nonfiction, *Regarding the Bathroom: A Privy to the Past*, by Kate

Klise (2006). Or, we could skip this step and move on to *Elijah of Buxton*, by Christopher Paul Curtis (2007a), and then to *Millions*, by Frank Cottrell Boyce (2004). From here, we can spring to the tongue-in-cheek humor of Lois Lowry's *Willoughbys* (2008), a fresh and funny take on the traditional orphan story that takes Lemony Snicket and ups the ante. The final rung is Derek Landy's deliciously sly *Skulduggery Pleasant* (2007). This detective mystery is hilarious and suspenseful. The voice of the main character, a private eye who just happens to be a skeleton, is captivating.

The audio production of this first book in the Skulduggery series was an Odyssey Honor winner for 2008, which serves as an excellent reminder not to neglect books in other media when constructing these ladders. Audiobooks, ebooks, graphic novels, and the like can make books more accessible to less skilled readers or to readers who are struggling with disabilities of all sorts. They provide another way to help students make stepping from one rung to another an easier task. And another reminder: don't limit the use of audiobooks, ebooks, and graphic novels to struggling readers only; they are appropriate and appreciated by readers of all ages and abilities. Later in the book, I talk more about audiobooks and even provide some audiobook reading ladders.

> Audiobooks, ebooks, graphic novels, and the like can make books more accessible to less skilled readers or to readers who are struggling with disabilities of all sorts.

Climbing a Few More Ladders

I worked on an interdisciplinary team of teachers for about a decade during my middle school teaching career. We planned together for our students so they could see the connections that existed from one content area to another. What I loved about this experience was the opportunity to share with my colleagues the wealth of books that could touch on the concepts and content of their classes. Since the reading portion of many state tests includes expository texts, I think it is a good idea to include nonfiction in what we offer our students. With that in mind, look at the two reading ladders in Figures 5.5 and 5.6; each includes content area connections.

Reading About a Historical Period

Figure 5.5 is a ladder with books all set sometime in the turbulent 1960s, an era of reform and revolt. In this instance, there are two bottom rungs—one for female readers and one for male readers. *Runaround* (Hemphill 2007), the pick for female

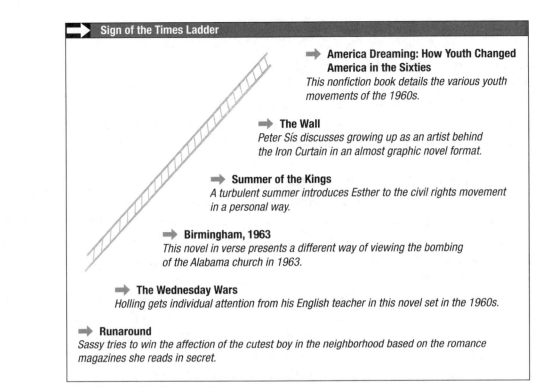

Sign of the Times Ladder

America Dreaming: How Youth Changed America in the Sixties
This nonfiction book details the various youth movements of the 1960s.

The Wall
Peter Sís discusses growing up as an artist behind the Iron Curtain in an almost graphic novel format.

Summer of the Kings
A turbulent summer introduces Esther to the civil rights movement in a personal way.

Birmingham, 1963
This novel in verse presents a different way of viewing the bombing of the Alabama church in 1963.

The Wednesday Wars
Holling gets individual attention from his English teacher in this novel set in the 1960s.

Runaround
Sassy tries to win the affection of the cutest boy in the neighborhood based on the romance magazines she reads in secret.

Figure 5.5 *Sign of the Times Ladder*

readers, is a coming-of-age story set in Kentucky. Eleven-year-old Sassy hates her older sister, has a crush on one of the cute town boys, and reads romance magazines on the sly. History serves simply as the backdrop for this story of first love and first betrayal. Sassy's male counterpart, Holling Hoodhood in Gary Schmidt's *Wednesday Wars* (2007), is not interested in romance. Instead, he and his seventh-grade English teacher, Mrs. Baker, spend a great deal of time together on Wednesday afternoons. These sessions lead Holling in directions he never dreamed possible. History plays a more active, albeit secondary, role in the story, with plenty of references to what is happening in the culture.

The final three books of this ladder deal more directly with what is occurring historically. *Birmingham*, by Carole Boston Weatherford (2007), is a free-verse, fictional account of the bombing of the Sixteenth Street Church by the Ku Klux Klan. It is the design of this slim, eloquent book that bears some study in this reading ladder; not only is this a novel in verse, but it is filled with collages that combine photos and facsimiles of news clippings from the era. Of course, there is a logical jumping-off point into Christopher Paul Curtis' *Watsons Go to Birmingham—1963* (1995) here as well.

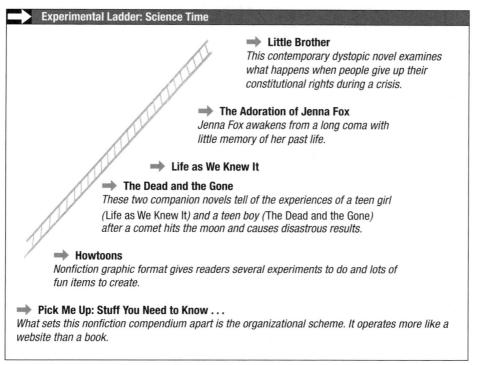

Experimental Ladder: Science Time

➡ **Little Brother**
This contemporary dystopic novel examines what happens when people give up their constitutional rights during a crisis.

➡ **The Adoration of Jenna Fox**
Jenna Fox awakens from a long coma with little memory of her past life.

➡ **Life as We Knew It**
➡ **The Dead and the Gone**
These two companion novels tell of the experiences of a teen girl
(Life as We Knew It) and a teen boy (The Dead and the Gone)
after a comet hits the moon and causes disastrous results.

➡ **Howtoons**
Nonfiction graphic format gives readers several experiments to do and lots of fun items to create.

➡ **Pick Me Up: Stuff You Need to Know . . .**
What sets this nonfiction compendium apart is the organizational scheme. It operates more like a website than a book.

Figure 5.6 *Experimental Ladder: Science Time*

Peter Sís' childhood behind the Iron Curtain is the subject of his Caldecott Honor Book *The Wall* (2007). Though its basic design is firmly rooted in the picture book, there are more than ample text and detailed illustrations that bring this historical era in another country to life. *A Summer of Kings*, by Han Nolan (2006), might tie nicely to the book on the bottom rung. It tells the story of a summer of changes, a summer in which fourteen-year-old Esther meets two young men named King. One is Martin Luther King Jr.; the other is an African American named King-Roy Johnson, who has been sent from Alabama to escape the horrors being visited on people in the South.

The top rung of our ladder is another informational book, *America Dreaming*, by Laban Carrick Hill (2007). Looking very much like a coffee table book in terms of format, the book is, in my opinion, more welcoming to reluctant readers than many nonfiction books. Its focus on how young people changed the course of history appeals to young adults, who are still quite egocentric. Social studies teachers will appreciate the information on the people and movements that helped make the '60s a time of radical change in America.

When constructing a reading ladder with historical fiction and informational books, it might not be necessary to use books with the same or similar settings in time and place. Instead, it could prove valuable to offer books set in widely distinct eras but with characters and themes that are similar. Kenny in *The Watsons Go to Birmingham—1963* (Curtis 1995) is in many ways as naïve as Bruno in John Boyne's *Boy in the Striped Pajamas* (2006), a novel set during the Holocaust. Whereas Kenny does not know how cruel humans can be to one another, Bruno does not even understand that the people he sees behind the fence are being held in a concentration camp.

If we continue with books set in other times, we can construct a reading ladder that includes *The Book Thief* (Zusak 2007), *Hattie Big Sky* (Larson 2006), *The Invention of Hugo Cabret* (Selznick 2007), and *London Calling* (Bloor 2006). Liesel, the heroine of Marcus Zusack's *Book Thief*, relies on the power of words and language to help her escape from the horror of Nazi Germany. Likewise, Hattie in Kirby Larson's *Hattie Big Sky* finds that writing about her isolation and the trials facing a lone woman in a Montana winter helps her deal with her difficulties; she, too, longs for companionship. Hugo Cabret, the title character from Brian Selznick's *Invention of Hugo Cabret*, wishes for family; Jimmy wants to save his family from the London bombings of World War II in *London Calling*. In all of these books, the main characters harbor feelings that should still resonate with contemporary readers: the wish for safety, for love, for acceptance.

INCORPORATING THE SCIENCES

The ladder in Figure 5.6 deals with the sciences. Our bottom rung, *Pick Me Up: Stuff You Need to Know . . .* (Roberts and Leslie 2006), combines the visual complexity of David Macaulay's *Way Things Work* (1988)—a book that could also be a part of this ladder—with the organizational influences of emerging illustrative styles and even shades of the Internet. Information is organized through links that are color-coded on the page, inviting readers to progress through the book by turning to other related topics rather than reading in a linear, sequential approach. Today's teens, the first generation to have grown up with plenty of access to information online, will appreciate this organizational scheme that connects information on da Vinci to information on supermodels.

Howtoons (Griffith 2007) is a book that incorporates the format of the graphic novel with the genre of nonfiction—in this case, the how-to book. Author Saul Griffith is an engineer and recipient of a MacArthur genius grant. He brings his scientific expertise to the pages of this book, detailing how to create marshmallow shooters from PVC pipe and a flute from a turkey baster.

On the next rung of this ladder, we leave nonfiction and enter into the realm of fiction in two books by Susan Beth Pfeffer: *Life as We Knew It* (2006) and *The Dead and the Gone* (2008). These two companion books cover the same event, but from the perspectives of two different characters in different locales. After a comet hits the moon and knocks it off course, life on planet Earth is tenuous. Crops fail, tidal waves consume cities, communication breaks down. In this postapocalyptic scenario, Pfeffer places two teens who must survive despite the odds and their inexperience. In *Life as We Knew It*, set in rural Pennsylvania, sixteen-year-old Miranda and her family fight to stay alive. *The Dead and the Gone* introduces readers to seventeen-year-old Alex, who must try to survive and protect his sisters in the heart of New York City. You could have students select one of the two books to read and then share their books with one another in literature circles. More often than not, this sharing leads the members of the group to read the other selection. I can still recall Brian's lament once: "It's not fair, Mrs. Lesesne; you make us want to read books we don't even have to!"

The final two rungs of this ladder are dystopic views of a not-too-distant future and seem to follow logically from the adventure and survival stories in the Pfeffer books. *The Adoration of Jenna Fox*, by Mary E. Pearson (2008), explores the field of medical ethics in a future where equal access to health care has become the law of the land. However, Jenna's parents have violated that law in order to save the life of their daughter who is horribly injured in a car accident. Jenna has no real memory of what has happened before the accident or even about her time in recovery from her injuries, and her discovery of the extent of her parents' interventions medically is nothing short of terrifying. *Little Brother*, by Cory Doctorow (2008), deals with a frightening scenario that is not too far from our current reality. How much freedom will people surrender in the name of fighting against terrorism? Other dystopic and futuristic novels could readily be added to this ladder, including *The Giver*, by Lois Lowry (2002), Peter Dickinson's *Eva* (1989), and *Feed*, by M. T. Anderson (2002).

* * *

We have now analyzed the purpose, logic, and construction of reading ladders, and we understand that our careful blending of genres, forms, format, and other techniques is key as we construct them. Now let's explore how to help our students achieve a smooth and steady ascent toward broader reading and understanding.

Upping the Ante with Reading Ladders

chapter

6

It should come as no surprise that I like to hang out in bookstores or that my friends share this hobby. One afternoon a few years ago, my friend Kylene Beers and I decided to visit a bookstore to see what was new and interesting. One of the titles we were both interested in exploring was Thomas Friedman's *World Is Flat* (2007). I purchased an audio copy; Kylene bought the hardcover. The book affected us both deeply and shifted our approach to our profession in some important ways. This title, along with Kylene's recommendation of Daniel Pink's *Whole New Mind* (2005), have pushed me to look at books and reading through a slightly different lens.

Pink and Friedman make some salient points about how to prepare our students for twenty-first-century literacies—points that also inform our move from basic reading ladders (like those we created in the previous chapter) to more complex ladders. Though neither author offers anything particularly new to education, they *have* found a wide audience outside of the education community, and that gives us a basis for initiating discussion with stakeholders outside of the profession. This may be the critical link that leads to real reform in our classrooms.

Though it is no simple task to coalesce the work of Friedman and Pink, I want to discuss how some of the basic concepts of their work inform us as we build reading ladders and, consequently, readers. I encourage educators to read (or listen to or download) these books and take away their implications for education.

Building with the Basics and Beyond

This book began with the metaphor of Lincoln Logs, exemplifying the concept of laying a foundation before building anything of substance. The first four chapters of this book serve to help us connect readers to books in basic, foundational ways. In the process, we have explored some basic materials we can use to construct reading ladders: some involve how we set up our classrooms; a few have to do with knowing which books will be best suited for our students; establishing top and bottom rungs is certainly one of the basics; and reading widely in the field of literature for children and young adults is a must. Once we have covered these basics and feel comfortable in constructing some reading ladders, it is time to move forward and push the boundaries a bit.

Friedman emphasizes the importance of collaboration and connectivity in his discussion of what our students need to be productive in the future. We must also help them develop higher-order thinking skills and produce meaningful content. (Of course, this idea that students should create rather than simply consume is not new at all. Joseph Renzulli and Irving Sato discussed this element of education more than two decades ago.) One way to implement these concepts in our classrooms is to have students create some reading ladders themselves. How can we work with our students so that they begin to think about the connections between and among books?

First, we need to model this thinking for our students. We can do this explicitly in the classroom by taking short pieces of literature and showing them how we think through a selection. Here is a three-step process that could take place in the classroom:

1. Project a story onto a screen.
2. Read the story aloud, pausing to comment when you see an association between this story and any other.
3. Use a sticky note, highlighter, or marginal annotation to indicate connections as you make them.

Having the story visible for all to see is important as we attempt to move students from thinking about their reading in a concrete fashion to a more abstract fashion. When students can see the words and the notations we make as we think aloud, it offers a model for their own attempts later. I would demonstrate several of these over the course of a week so that students could see that connections are not limited to theme or plot or character, but are made through a wide range of possibilities. Here are a few variations on this strategy.

"Priscilla and the Wimps," a short story by Richard Peck (1984) from the collection *Sixteen*, edited by Don Gallo, is one place to start. In the story, Priscilla takes on the school bully, Monk Klutter. By the end of the tale, she has locked Klutter into a locker on a Friday afternoon. There is a blizzard over the weekend that closes down the school for a week. End of story. I use this story because the ending is reminiscent of the endings we see in stories by O. Henry and Saki. I can tie this story to "The Gift of the Magi" or "The Ransom of Red Chief" or "The Open Window." Tying a contemporary story to a classic is one connection we can demonstrate. Of course, we can also discuss contemporary works with surprising endings, such as *Tenderness*, by Robert Cormier (1997), or *Looking for Alaska*, by John Green (2005).

Other short stories can, of course, be substituted with different connections and rungs. In fact, using a different short story every day for a week should help solidify the process for students. Here, then, are some suggestions for the remainder of the week.

Day two could begin with reading aloud the story "The Mask of Eamonn Tiyado" (2008) from Bruce Coville's collection *Oddest of All*. The connection is, I hope, apparent from the play on words in Coville's title. Linking this story to Poe's "Cask of Amontillado" is a simple step. This approach might lead to a discussion of the components of the horror story. Other connections to short stories, both classic and contemporary, could be made here. Another possibility would be to tie into another medium and discuss how M. Night Shyamalan creates tension in movies such as *The Sixth Sense*.

For day three, our selection might be a survival story that we could tie to "To Build a Fire" or other classics. Consider a contemporary story, such as "The Last Book in the Universe," by Rodman Philbrick (1999). Philbrick later used this short story as the basis for a full-length work with the same title (2000).

"A Reasonable Sum," by Gordon Korman (1989) starts off day four. This humorous short story centers on an experience familiar to our students: the responsibility for caring for textbooks. After the students make connections (and I think they cannot help but do so in this story), take a few moments and ask them to create categories for the types of comments and connections they made to the text. You are now making them aware that there is more than one way to connect, to respond, to react to one particular text.

Finally, we can have students compare and contrast two short stories by the same author and with the same title. Chris Crutcher's collection *Athletic Shorts* (1991) contains two stories titled "The Pin." They share the same topic, title, and author yet are unique. We have now moved from a fairly concrete approach to a more abstract and complex one. Since we have compiled similarities and differences with this pairing, we have also demonstrated to students that opposites or differences can create connections between stories.

At the end of this week of sharing short stories, ask students to create reading ladders using the short stories from the class. They should assign a story to the top and the bottom rungs and then arrange the other three stories within this frame. Accompanying each ladder should be a paragraph or two explaining why the student placed each story on its respective rung. With any luck, there should be some variety in where students placed the five stories, giving rise to a discussion about the fact that there is no best way to arrange them. It also demonstrates that personal preferences and interests play a role in the creation of reading ladders. Another possible assignment would be to ask students to use one of the stories shared in class to develop a separate reading ladder focusing on theme or character or some other element of the story. Emphasize that this story could occupy any rung of the ladder.

Instead of or in addition to short stories, poems offer short texts that can be utilized to model this process for our students. Roald Dahl penned several humorous retellings of fairy tales in books such as *Revolting Rhymes* (2002). Sharing a poem (e.g., "Little Red Riding Hood and the Wolf") can lead to a discussion of the similarities and differences between versions of stories. Students could compare and contrast the Disney version of *Cinderella* with that of the Brothers Grimm.

Of course, there are plenty of other resources for terrific poems to use with tweens and teens. Since poetry can be quite abstract, I prefer to begin with some concrete poems. John Grandits' two collections are ideal for this purpose. *Technically, It's Not My Fault* (2004) and *Blue Lipstick* (2007) offer poems in a myriad of shapes. We can move students from these concrete poems to more abstract forms, such as those in Adam Rex's *Frankenstein Takes the Cake* (2008), a poetry collection that combines light and humorous verses with the graphic novel format. Included in this collection are blogs by the Headless Horseman and three selections titled "Edgar Allan Poem" that mimic the rhythm and rhyme scheme of "The Raven" to create clever parodies. As you did with the short stories, you can ask students to arrange the poems from one of these collections on reading ladders.

Opening chapters can provide another opportunity for us to engage students in the creation of reading ladders using relatively short selections of text. Table 6.1

OPENING CHAPTERS LADDER	
Middle School Titles	**High School Titles**
Bucking the Sarge (Curtis 2004)	*Looking for Alaska* (Green 2005)
Twilight (Meyer 2005)	*The Adoration of Jenna Fox* (Pearson 2008)
Millions (Cottrell Boyce 2004)	*The Compound* (Bodeen 2008)
Mysterious Benedict Society (Stewart 2007)	*Identical* (Hopkins 2008)
The London Eye Mystery (Dowd 2008)	*Little Brother* (Doctorow 2008)
Found (Haddix 2008)	*Generation Dead* (Waters 2008)
The Sky Inside (Dunkle 2008)	*Dead Is the New Black* (Perez 2008)
Watsons Go to Birmingham—1963 (Curtis 1995)	*Paper Towns* (Green 2008)
The Willoughbys (Lowry 2008)	*The Hunger Games* (Collins 2008)
The Underneath (Appelt 2008)	*He Forgot to Say Goodbye* (Saenz 2008)

Table 6.1 *Opening Chapters Ladder*

provides ten titles of books for high school and middle school whose opening chapters are riveting in some way: humorous, mysterious, suspenseful. After students have read all the opening paragraphs, they can again be asked to create ladders and to explain their selections. Use these guiding questions to generate discussion and writing:

- Consider the different ways to make connections between and among books. Will you make connections based on events from the stories? On similarities between and among the characters? On themes and issues? Personal associations? What other attributes might you consider?

- How will you determine the top and bottom rungs? What factors do you consider? How is one text more accessible or easier than the one above it? How do books on the lower rungs differ from those at the top?

- Do all the books on the reading ladder have the same intended audience? Are there factors that limit which books will appeal to which segments of the class? What are those factors?

Developing New Ways of Thinking About Text

In *A Whole New Mind*, Daniel Pink (2005) describes six elements that he believes are crucial to extending right-brained thinking: meaning, play, empathy, symphony, story, and design. Each of these elements carries with it emotions, experiences, and connections that will be unique to each student. In the figures that appear throughout this chapter, these elements come to life in a series of reading ladders constructed of several book titles. How those titles relate to each other and how one segues to the next is explained in the text. It is critical to note, however, that students will undoubtedly construct their ladders differently, and the most interesting part of the exercise is to discover why. Pink highlights six elements he believes are important for twenty-first-century learners: let's explore how these elements interact with the concept of reading ladders.

MEANING AND PLAY: LADDERS WITH TWO SENSES

Wordplay can elude students because figurative language is abstract in its nature. Often, this abstraction confounds readers who are concrete learners. Picture books, with their predictable form and format, are excellent tools for introducing students to wordplay and helping them grasp the meaning of similes, metaphors, and the like. Figures 6.1a and 6.1b are examples of the sense of play and, to some extent, meaning. The reading ladder in Figure 6.1a begins with picture books and ends

> In *A Whole New Mind*, Daniel Pink (2005) describes six elements that he believes are crucial to extending right-brained thinking: meaning, play, empathy, symphony, story, and design.

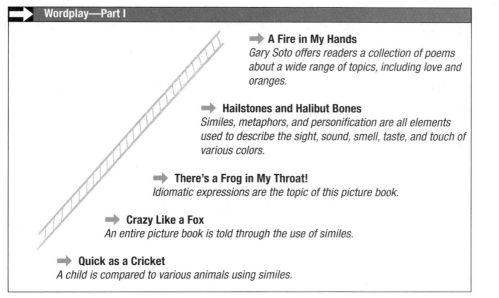

Wordplay—Part I

➡ **A Fire in My Hands**
Gary Soto offers readers a collection of poems about a wide range of topics, including love and oranges.

➡ **Hailstones and Halibut Bones**
Similes, metaphors, and personification are all elements used to describe the sight, sound, smell, taste, and touch of various colors.

➡ **There's a Frog in My Throat!**
Idiomatic expressions are the topic of this picture book.

➡ **Crazy Like a Fox**
An entire picture book is told through the use of similes.

➡ **Quick as a Cricket**
A child is compared to various animals using similes.

Figure 6.1a *Wordplay—Part I*

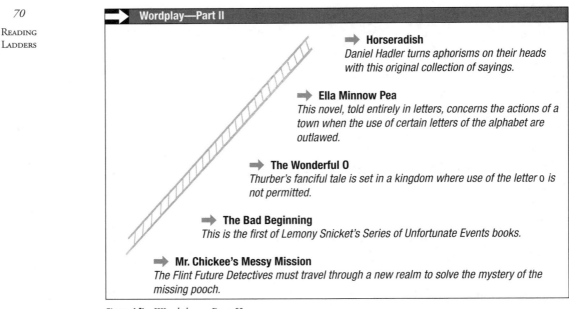

Wordplay—Part II

➡️ **Horseradish**
Daniel Hadler turns aphorisms on their heads with this original collection of sayings.

➡️ **Ella Minnow Pea**
This novel, told entirely in letters, concerns the actions of a town when the use of certain letters of the alphabet are outlawed.

➡️ **The Wonderful O**
Thurber's fanciful tale is set in a kingdom where use of the letter o is not permitted.

➡️ **The Bad Beginning**
This is the first of Lemony Snicket's Series of Unfortunate Events books.

➡️ **Mr. Chickee's Messy Mission**
The Flint Future Detectives must travel through a new realm to solve the mystery of the missing pooch.

Figure 6.1b *Wordplay—Part II*

with two poetry collections. Figure 6.1b's reading ladder contains books that feature language at play.

The ability to use language figuratively is crucial to the development of writing skills; it is also a critical element of advanced literacy. Scores on the National Assessment of Educational Progress indicate that most of our middle and high school students are unable to read beyond the basic level. Identifying figurative language and other devices is a skill proficient readers possess. How do we assist our students in identifying these devices and using them appropriately? These reading ladders present a two-pronged approach.

Audrey Wood's *Quick as a Cricket* (1994) is a simple rhymed text that uses similes comparing children to various animals. Similes are also the emphasis in Loreen Leedy's *Crazy Like a Fox* (2008), allowing us to present multiple examples of how similes are constructed. Additionally, Leedy provides instructions in the back matter of the book to guide students in constructing their own simile stories. Idioms, another difficult literary device, are the focus of *There's a Frog in My Throat!* (Leedy 2003). Similes, metaphors, personification, and hyperbole are some of the figurative devices used in this picture book.

The final two books in this reading ladder are books of poetry. *Hailstones and Halibut Bones*, by Mary O'Neill (1989), presents poems about different colors. The use of figurative language is rich and accessible, a rare combination. It is accessible in large part because the poems are about a topic students know well. Gary Soto's *Fire in My Hands* (2006) is an exquisite book of poetry, rich in literary devices and yet still accessible to readers, as the poems discuss baseball, love, and other topics within students' realm of experience. Notice that as we progress through this ladder, we move from humorous to more serious subject matter and treatments, and from very concrete examples of figurative language—in large part assisted by the illustrations of the picture books—to the more abstract examples in the poetry collections. Here, it is the subject matter that provides the scaffolding for readers.

The second reading ladder for wordplay uses more traditional texts at its base and ends with a rather unique offering from one of the masters of wordplay, Lemony Snicket (aka Daniel Hadler). *Mr. Chickee's Messy Mission*, by Christopher Paul Curtis (2007b), is a middle-grade novel about three children who solve mysteries in their Flint, Michigan, neighborhood. Their mission in this story involves traveling to an alternate universe inhabited by authors and their not fully realized creations. We need to share some of their adventures with students and point out the references to authors as diverse as Zora Neale Hurston and J. K. Rowling. On to Lemony Snicket's *The Bad Beginning* (2007a), the first in his Series of Unfortunate Events. The language is rich and, in some cases, archaic. What Snicket does so well is use context to assist readers in comprehending the vocabulary that might not be within their normal range.

The Wonderful O, by James Thurber (1990), is a classic that will, more than likely, be unfamiliar to contemporary readers. When the letter *o* is removed from words as a punishment to the residents of a town, confusion and hilarity ensue. Imagine life without this letter. *Ella Minnow Pea*, by Mark Dunn (2001), takes Thurber and ups the ante. In the town of Nollopville, residents must cope with losing more and more letters of the alphabet. This story, told entirely in letters written by the villagers to those outside of Nollopville, becomes a cryptic puzzle as one by one the use of letters—alphabet letters, that is—is outlawed. Now, in the place of the outlawed letters are asterisks. Readers will have to use all sorts of skills, from using context clues to inferring to just plain guessing in some instances, in order to follow the chain of events. This reading ladder could take some different directions along the way.

For example, *The Phantom Tollbooth*, by Norton Juster (1996), could readily follow the selection by Thurber or by Dunn. In this instance, however, we have Lemony Snicket's *Horseradish* (2007b). Subtitled *Bitter Truths You Can't Avoid*, this book is a compendium of axioms that are unlikely to become as famous as some from *Poor Richard's Almanac*. Instead, Snicket skewers the form with some new offerings about education, about relationships, about life. Snicket has created new clichés for students to examine.

Let's investigate for a moment some possible alternatives to the reading ladders in Figures 6.1a and 6.1b. One English as a second language (ESL or ELL) class took a detour after reading the picture book *There's a Frog in My Throat!* Students were fascinated with idiomatic expressions, those turns of phrases that so often confound those new to English. The teacher reported, "It was like seeing lightbulbs go off over the students' heads as they realized English did not always mean exactly what the words said." A discussion about idioms led them to some other reading. In this case, the class enjoyed some variations of the Cinderella story from different cultures, beginning with *Bubba the Cowboy Prince* (Ketteman 1997) and culminating with *Mufaro's Beautiful Daughters* (Steptoe 1987), an African version of the tale. The class created one large reading ladder with a variety of Cinderella stories. Second and third reading ladders grouped stories they felt shared sufficient similarities. Finally, they sectioned off a piece of their word wall for idiomatic expressions they encountered in and outside of school.

Similes, metaphors, and other forms of language play are the focus of each of these ladders. The top rung of the ladder in Figure 6.1a could easily become the first rung of the ladder in Figure 6.1b. Building from relatively simple examples to more complex uses of figurative language easily takes students from the concrete to the abstract. One class used *Hailstones and Halibut Bones* as a model for writing its own poems. Instead of colors, the class brainstormed other concepts that might be described in poetic forms. Groups of students then worked collaboratively on poems about numbers, letters of the alphabet, and even geometric figures.

As students become more conversant with wordplay, we can ask them to identify its implementation in passages from a variety of works. Mount a ladder of figurative language on the classroom wall and encourage students to bring in examples found in newspapers, magazines, blogs, and the like. They can affix each example to an index card with an explication of the example and some rationale for where they are placing it along the rungs. One class found that the evening news programs yielded a great many examples, especially ones that involved hyperbole. Interestingly enough, these examples were all placed along the bottom rungs of the figurative language ladder! After students dealt with hyperbole, the teacher shared *Bat Boy Lives!* (Perel and the editors of the *Weekly World News* 2005), a nonfiction book featuring headlines from the *Weekly World News* about Elvis sightings and other incredible phenomena. This book led to an investigation of *Guinness World Records* (Guinness World Records Limited 2009), *Every Minute on Earth* (Murrie and Murrie 2007), and other books with bits of interesting factual trivia. This, in turn,

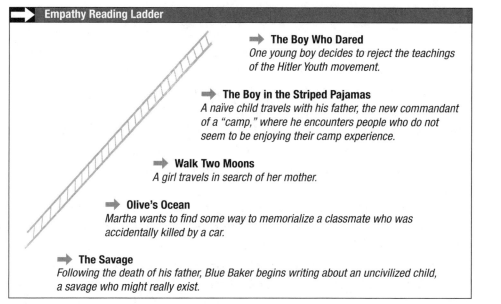

Empathy Reading Ladder

The Boy Who Dared
One young boy decides to reject the teachings of the Hitler Youth movement.

The Boy in the Striped Pajamas
A naïve child travels with his father, the new commandant of a "camp," where he encounters people who do not seem to be enjoying their camp experience.

Walk Two Moons
A girl travels in search of her mother.

Olive's Ocean
Martha wants to find some way to memorialize a classmate who was accidentally killed by a car.

The Savage
Following the death of his father, Blue Baker begins writing about an uncivilized child, a savage who might really exist.

Figure 6.2 *Empathy Reading Ladder*

led to Kadir Nelson's *We Are the Ship* (2008) and a new ladder of nonfiction selections.

EMPATHY

Empathy is stronger than sympathy, because it comes from our own experiences. Once we have lived through an event or experience, we know the feelings associated with it more intimately. For instance, if a student has been the target of name-calling, he tends to be more empathetic toward others who are experiencing the same fate. Books, too, can help develop empathy in readers. As we connect with the characters, we come to empathize with their feelings.

Reading ladders based on books through which this kind of theme runs can help students deal with the realities of their own or others' lives. As the books delve more deeply into the themes and the characters who experience them, students' capacity to internalize someone else's feelings or to recognize and deal with their own feelings expands, pushing them toward a broader and more humane understanding of their world. Figure 6.2 is one example of such a ladder—in this case, based on empathy. Follow the reasoning behind this kind of ladder, and think about how it or similar ladders could support and sensitize your students.

In David Almond's *The Savage* (2008), Blue Baker comes face-to-face with a savage boy, a boy who dares to do all the things the main character cannot. This graphic novel might give some readers a sense of empowerment. Others might be able to deal with loss more effectively, while still others might realize the need to be a supportive sibling. *Olive's Ocean*, by Kevin Henkes (2003), can help readers in the throes of first love or first rejection or the loss of a peer. Loss is also central to *Walk Two Moons*, by Sharon Creech (1994), as Salamanca Tree Hiddle (call her Sal, please) searches for her mother. And both of these books contain an intergenerational family relationship. *Bridge to Terabithia* (Paterson 2007) could easily fit in here, too.

The final two books on this ladder take a bit of a turn from contemporary fiction to historical and informational literature. *The Boy in the Striped Pajamas*, by John Boyne (2006), is an allegory about the Holocaust. Our main character is a naïve young child who believes he and his parents are moving from their home so that his father can supervise a new camp. Of course, when they arrive, this young boy is puzzled: Why do the people at the camp seem so unhappy? Isn't camp supposed to be fun? Careful readers will pick up on the historical setting and situation. However, they will not be prepared for the incredible twist awaiting them near the end of the novel. A small side step in this ladder might be to have students view the movie made from this remarkable novel. After viewing, the class could brainstorm two additional ladders—one that notes the similarities between novel and movie and another that notes the differences; these ladders will no doubt generate an interesting discussion.

Susan Campbell Bartoletti's *The Boy Who Dared* (2008) is a novel that comes from the research she conducted for *Hitler Youth* (2005). It is essentially a novel based on an actual person, a young man who initially enlists in the Hitler Youth. Soon, though, he comes to understand the fallacy that underlies this organization. Before long, he is writing in protest of all that is transpiring around him. He is arrested and, after refusing to recant his position, sentenced to death. This is a story of heroism in the face of incredible personal danger. Dozens of other books could easily be fashioned into connecting ladders that have at their core the selfless sacrifice of one individual and the impact one person can have.

Notice, also, the leaps we have made in the original ladder, going from a graphic-type novel for intermediate readers to middle-grade novels and, ultimately, to historical stories. The books have grown more complex; the situations with which readers are asked to identify are increasingly difficult and abstract. We are growing readers as we progress through this ladder. Further, not one of the books on this

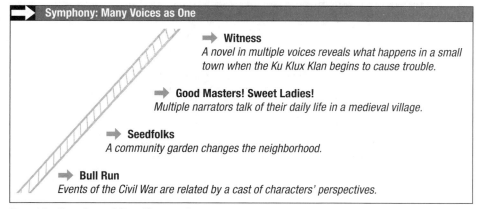

Figure 6.3a *Symphony: Many Voices as One*

ladder is simplistic in its construction. All the books demand active reading. Each should also lead to some interesting writing prompts, such as the following:

- How are Sal from *Walk Two Moons* and Martha from *Olive's Ocean* similar? Different?

- What would happen if we were to switch the main characters of *The Boy in the Striped Pajamas* and *The Boy Who Dared*?

- Describe what a day would be like for one of the characters from *Olive's Ocean*, *The Savage*, or *The Boy Who Dared* if he or she were to take Sal's advice and walk a mile in someone else's shoes.

- Write about a time when you had to take an unpopular stand, a time when you had to accept the consequences for something you had done, or a time when you witnessed an injustice.

SYMPHONY

When I hear the word *symphony*, I literally hear the opening strains of an orchestra. I think of how the various instruments blend to create one effect. So it is with the books in Figures 6.3a and 6.3b. The books blend either in form, format, or plot element to create a ladder that is greater than the sum of its parts.

Notice that in these two ladders, we have fewer titles. That is not because of a dearth of books with multiple narrators or points of view. Rather, I narrowed the focus of these two ladders substantially as we consider the concept of symphony. This does not mean, though, that more elaborate ladders could not be constructed.

Bull Run (1993) and *Seedfolks* (2004) are both by Paul Fleischman. In *Bull Run*, the events leading up to the first battle of the Civil War are related from the

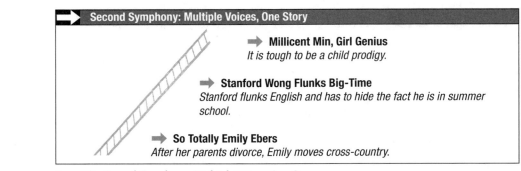

Figure 6.3b *Second Symphony: Multiple Voices, One Story*

perspective of a young soldier from the South, a woman rolling bandages for soldiers in a battle far from her home, couriers running between generals, and myriad others. *Seedfolks* has a contemporary setting—a garden in the city that is being tended by the residents of the neighborhood. What both books have in common is that everyone has a slightly different take on the same series of events. Individuals tend to filter perceptions through experience.

I talked earlier in this book about the Newbery-winning *Good Masters! Sweet Ladies! Voices from a Medieval Village* (Schlitz 2007). Schlitz's use of multiple voices gives readers a well-rounded idea of life in this village. *Witness*, by Karen Hesse (2001), utilizes multiple narrators to relate the events in a small town in Vermont in the 1920s when the Ku Klux Klan attempts to infiltrate it.

There are certainly other books with multiple narrators. A possible start for a reading ladder for older readers might include *Nick and Norah's Infinite Playlist*, by Rachel Cohn and David Levithan (2006), *Slake's Limbo*, by Felice Holman (1986), *The Pigman*, by Paul Zindel (2005), or *The Realm of Possibility*, by David Levithan (2006). Younger readers could be pointed to the collaborative works of Ann M. Martin and Paula Danziger, *P.S. Longer Letter Later* (1998) and *Snail Mail No More* (2000). Three novels by Lauren Myracle, *Ttyl* (2004), *Ttfn* (2006), and *L8r, G8r* (2007), are also perfect for a ladder. Written entirely in emails and IMs among three teen girls, these books could also be featured in a ladder about design.

The second reading ladder for symphony contains three titles by Lisa Yee. In *Millicent Min, Girl Genius* (2003), Millie is an eleven-year-old genius taking high school classes and tutoring family friend Stanford Wong. When Millie meets Emily, she does not tell her new friend that she is a genius. When Emily discovers the deception, her feelings are hurt. Millie comes to realize that Emily is hurt, not because

Millie is smart, but because Millie did not trust her friend enough to tell the truth. The subsequent books by Yee, *Stanford Wong Flunks Big-Time* (2005) and *So Totally Emily Ebers* (2007), relate this same time period of events from the perspective of the other players involved. Because these three novels all center on the same set of characters but are told from different perspectives, the order of the books on the ladder is not as crucial. You might elect to have students read the books in the order in which they were published (*Millicent Min, Stanford Wong, Emily Ebers*) or in any order you desire.

A Different Sort of Symphony: Audiobooks

Admit it: You or some of your colleagues think listening to a book is cheating in some way. In 2008, an article in *The New York Times* book section asserted just this. However, as someone who has learned to read with her ears, I can assure you that listening to an audiobook can be just as engaged an experience as reading text. The American Library Association developed a new award for audiobooks, the Odyssey Award, first presented in 2008. As a member of that inaugural committee, I listened to hundreds of hours of children's and YA books in audio format. I became more attuned to voice, pitch, tone, narrative style, and other elements of audio. If I had read the book before listening to the audio production, in many cases I heard something I had missed in my reading of the text. Symphony, to me, suggests the beautiful melding and blending of various sounds: audiobooks do just that. And so, Figure 6.3c is a reading ladder for audiobooks.

> However, as someone who has learned to read with her ears, I can assure you that listening to an audiobook can be just as engaged an experience as reading text.

Begin your students' listening experience with *Seven Blind Mice*. Written by Ed Young (2007) and narrated by B. D. Wong, this audiobook is, first, short, allowing time to listen to it in its entirety and enter into discussion within the same class period. After students have listened to the book, show them the book with its illustrations. During the discussion have students compare and contrast these two very different media. Which is more effective and why? Which did they prefer and why? Then introduce the audio version of Walter Dean Myers' *Jazz* (2008a) by playing two of the tracks. I would suggest "Old Bob Johnson" as one selection. The reading of the poem is accompanied by the thrums of a New Orleans–style funeral procession complete with music and mourners. The last line of the poem is sung. Talk with students here might center around simple concepts such as the rhythm of the poem and word choices made by Myers. Follow this track up with "BeBop" to

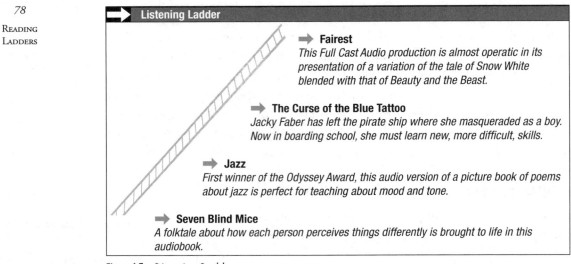

Listening Ladder

➡️ **Fairest**
This Full Cast Audio production is almost operatic in its presentation of a variation of the tale of Snow White blended with that of Beauty and the Beast.

➡️ **The Curse of the Blue Tattoo**
Jacky Faber has left the pirate ship where she masqueraded as a boy. Now in boarding school, she must learn new, more difficult, skills.

➡️ **Jazz**
First winner of the Odyssey Award, this audio version of a picture book of poems about jazz is perfect for teaching about mood and tone.

➡️ **Seven Blind Mice**
A folktale about how each person perceives things differently is brought to life in this audiobook.

Figure 6.3c *Listening Ladder*

demonstrate how rhythm changes depending on the subject matter of the poem. Listen to the distinctive narrative styles to talk about voice. How does the music establish a mood and tone quite different from "Old Bob Johnson"? Dialect, accent, and other narrative factors can also be a part of the discussion.

For the audiobooks on the top two rungs of the ladder, we can extend our discussion to include other factors such as pacing, pitch, tone, volume, and the like. Accent and dialect still play roles in these two audiobooks as well. *The Curse of the Blue Tattoo*, by L. A. Meyer (2008) and narrated by Katherine Kellgren, is the second installment in the story of Jacky Faber, a young girl who masquerades as a boy to gain employment on a British frigate. This second book takes place after Jacky's sham has been uncovered. She is put off the ship and sent to a boarding school to learn skills more fitting for a young woman. Kellgren, an able narrator, handles accents that range from the poor British girl Jacky to the privileged attendees at the colonial American boarding school. Jacky is a performer as well, earning some money singing in the saloons. Kellgren's skilled vocals add a layer to Jacky Faber's character that would never be heard in a traditional reading of the novel. Likewise, *Fairest*, by Gail Carson Levine (2007), relies on music for an essential part of the plot. Asa has one of the finest voices in her village but feels she is an ugly young woman. When she ends up at the court of the king and his new queen, Asa's ability to throw her voice (she calls it illusing) allows the new queen to present herself as skilled in song, something prized by the kingdom. Hearing the voice of Asa and some of the other players reinforces their characters. Give students the opening chapters of each of the two books and ask them to read silently, making notes in the margins about anything that confuses them or causes them to pause. Then, play the opening chapter of each book, asking students to make a note of anything that strikes them (good or bad). Which did they prefer and why? What was difficult in the reading? In the listening?

Books that involve dialect and accents and foreign settings (including the past or a fantasy setting) are often better understood in audio format. Allowing students to hear the accents and dialects can help them navigate the sometimes difficult text. Other books that might be placed in this ladder include *Elijah of Buxton*, by Christopher Paul Curtis (2008), itself an Odyssey Honor audiobook; *Nightjohn*, by Gary Paulsen (1993); and *Treasure Island*, by Robert Louis Stevenson (2007), another Odyssey Honor winner. The list of Odyssey winners is available at the YALSA website (www.ala.org/yalsa). Also note there is an "Amazing Audiobooks" list with productions suitable for teens.

DESIGN

Visual literacy is a key twenty-first-century skill. It involves, in part, the ability to interpret an image—that is, to make meaning from the image. Drawings, paintings, and other images can be read and discussed just as texts are. Since much of the information we take in each and every day is visual, and since the Internet has become a place where many of our students spend considerable time reading, it is imperative that we provide some instruction in how to read images. Design is just one component of visual literacy. It is a concept that can be developed through observation and analysis of books. The simplest place to begin is with picture books. Their brief length (most are thirty-two pages) makes them ideal for in-class use and study.

The first reading ladder on design (Figure 6.4a) contains a handful of picture books in which color plays a key role. We could just as easily include books that focus on the use of line or shape or perspective. One terrific resource for teachers who wish to learn more about how to examine picture books in terms of design is Molly Bang's *Picture This! Perception and Composition* (1991), which details components of design including line, shape, color, and perspective. The text in the book is minimal, but the simple yet eloquent examples of how each of these components affects how we read images is instructive for students of all ages.

Olivia, by Ian Falconer (2000), uses back-and-white illustrations with just tinges of red—an effective use of the color element of design—to tell the story of a pig named Olivia and her escapades. This limited use of red helps draw the reader's

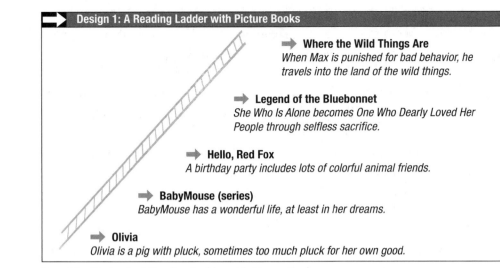

Design 1: A Reading Ladder with Picture Books

➡ **Where the Wild Things Are**
*When Max is punished for bad behavior, he
travels into the land of the wild things.*

➡ **Legend of the Bluebonnet**
*She Who Is Alone becomes One Who Dearly Loved Her
People through selfless sacrifice.*

➡ **Hello, Red Fox**
A birthday party includes lots of colorful animal friends.

➡ **BabyMouse (series)**
BabyMouse has a wonderful life, at least in her dreams.

➡ **Olivia**
Olivia is a pig with pluck, sometimes too much pluck for her own good.

Figure 6.4a *Design 1: A Reading Ladder with Picture Books*

eye to the most important object or action on the page. Students could be asked to transfer this knowledge about the use of color to their textbooks, to websites they browse, and to other objects in their environment. Jennifer and Matthew Holm's (2005) heroine BabyMouse is much like Olivia in that she is rather sure of herself but certainly has her problems in life. Black-and-white illustrations in this series of graphic novels for young readers are highlighted by BabyMouse's favorite color: pink. Ask students why Olivia prefers red while BabyMouse prefers pink. See if they can make the connection in the two colors.

Hello, Red Fox, by Eric Carle (1998), makes a very unique use of color. In this story, readers are asked to stare at a boldly colored animal and then at a blank page where they will see, thanks to a phenomenon called simultaneous contrast after-image, the animal in a complementary color. Complementary colors might be a new concept to many students, but certainly not to graphic designers and those who create and craft websites and ad campaigns.

Tomie dePaola's *Legend of the Bluebonnet* (1983) uses colors in a more subtle way. In this Native American legend, dePaola's palette reflects the dust and arid nature of the land in drought. The blues are all shades found within the flower that will spread across Texas, thanks to the generosity of One Who Dearly Loved Her People.

The master of design in picture books must be Maurice Sendak. *Where the Wild Things Are* (1991) remains one of the best-selling children's books more than forty years after its initial publication. It can be used to teach so many elements of art and design, including the essential element of color. Note how, as the mood changes, the colors shift to reflect that change; a palette of earthy tones—blues, greens, reds, and browns—dominates. Texture is added to the illustrations via cross-hatching and other techniques and engages the reader with an almost tactile experience.

There are literally hundreds of picture books that could be used in reading ladders. Just because the intended audience is young does not mean these books cannot offer a rich and rewarding experience for students in middle school, high school, and beyond. I often use them for quick read-alouds, to introduce a concept or theme, or as a writing prompt.

A logical extension of children's love of picture books is reflected in the growing popularity of the graphic novel format, the focus of the ladder in Figure 6.4b. *The Stonekeeper* (2008), the first book in Kazu Kibuishi's Amulet series, introduces

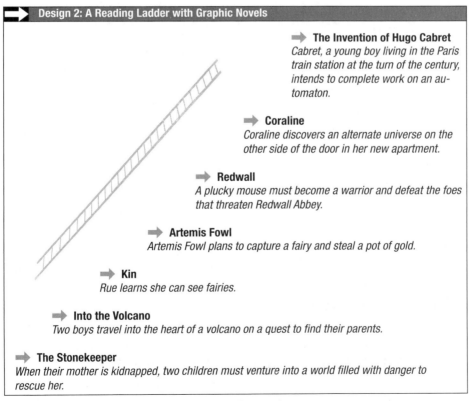

Design 2: A Reading Ladder with Graphic Novels

➡ **The Invention of Hugo Cabret**
Cabret, a young boy living in the Paris train station at the turn of the century, intends to complete work on an automaton.

➡ **Coraline**
Coraline discovers an alternate universe on the other side of the door in her new apartment.

➡ **Redwall**
A plucky mouse must become a warrior and defeat the foes that threaten Redwall Abbey.

➡ **Artemis Fowl**
Artemis Fowl plans to capture a fairy and steal a pot of gold.

➡ **Kin**
Rue learns she can see fairies.

➡ **Into the Volcano**
Two boys travel into the heart of a volcano on a quest to find their parents.

➡ **The Stonekeeper**
When their mother is kidnapped, two children must venture into a world filled with danger to rescue her.

Figure 6.4b *Design 2: A Reading Ladder with Graphic Novels*

readers to Emily, a young girl who has moved into a rather spooky family home. There she discovers a magic amulet left behind by her great-grandfather. Emily will need the amulet to unlock secrets, including the location of her kidnapped mother. *The Stonekeeper* combines light fantasy with the illustrations used in *manga*, the Japanese word for comics and an increasingly popular genre in the United States. Manga utilizes shapes and colors in symbolic fashion, which ties it nicely to the picture book format. Students can be instructed to examine the illustrations for examples of symbolism, a first step in helping them to locate symbolism within other texts. Note that this ladder could take a sideways thrust and explore nonfiction titles about manga and anime illustration. However, for now, we want to emphasize the concept of design.

The next rung, then, is Don Wood's *Into the Volcano* (2008). Wood is a Caldecott-winning illustrator who has often looked for ways to push the illustration envelope. A quick examination of the cover alone will provide food for discussion. Wood has opted for several panels instead of one large illustration. Why this choice? Ask students to notice the color palette here, too, as the colors not only provide mood and tone for the story but also reflect the setting.

Holly Black is no stranger to the field of YA literature or children's literature. As a matter of fact, her books—from The Spiderwick Chronicles to the urban fairy stories in *Tithe* (2004) and *Valiant* (2006)—could be at the opposite ends of the ladder, with *Kin* (2008) in the center of the ladder. In *Kin*—part of The Good Neighbors, her new series in graphic novel format—color, or the lack thereof, is still an essential element of design. Illustrative style differences between this selection and the ones by Wood and Kibuishi could also become a focus for discussion.

The books in the middle of this reading ladder, *Artemis Fowl* (Colfer and Donkin 2007), *Coraline* (Gaiman 2008a), and *Redwall* (Jacques 2007), are graphic novel adaptations of already published books. Because these books have already been published in a traditional format, it begs the question: Why offer readers the same story in a different format? What could be gained or lost with this change? None of these books has been illustrated by its author. Some books are not adapted by the original author. Does that change the story in some way?

Here is another example of where the reading ladder could take an unexpected turn, and students might elect to break into groups and read both versions of the book. There are other books undergoing this transformation from traditional to graphic, as well. The Pendragon series by MacHale, the Baby-Sitters Club series by Ann Martin, and even Nancy Drew are all available in this new format. Add to this the offerings by new imprints that are graphic novel adaptations of the classics

(Gareth Hinds' *Beowulf* [2007] and *The Merchant of Venice* [2008] or the Puffin Graphics versions of *Frankenstein* [Reed 2005] and *MacBeth* [Cover 2005], for instance), and many other reading ladders are suddenly possible.

Last, but by no means least, on this reading ladder is the groundbreaking and Caldecott-winning novel *The Invention of Hugo Cabret*, by Brian Selznick (2007). In his Caldecott speech, Selznick revealed that his inspiration for *Hugo Cabret* was the Remy Charlip classic children's book *Fortunately*. Selznick wanted to create a book in which the action on one page caused the action that followed on the next. He did this by marrying the textless picture book with the traditional novel. Throughout the more than five hundred pages of the novel, Selznick moves effortlessly between textless spreads of black-and-white illustrations and pages of traditional chapters of text. The illustrations do more than elaborate on the text, however. In this case, the illustrations continue to tell the story and advance the plot. It is a seamless dance and certainly a book in which design plays a key role. One suggestion for an addition to the study of this book might be to grab hold of the audiobook version, as it comes with a stunning DVD in which Selznick explains his approach to the design and structure of the novel.

A Final Thought

Consider the array of books that have found places on the rungs of these reading ladders. Picture books, poetry, nonfiction, graphic novels, and historical fiction have all made appearances, as have fantasy, realistic fiction, and even traditional literature and classics. Truly, the possibilities are endless. Ladders can move along in different directions and morph into something else (book webs? book scaffolds?). The only limitations have to do with the number of books we as educators can access and include.

> Ladders can move along in different directions and morph into something else (book webs? book scaffolds?).

And that leads me to one final consideration: finding time to read. Over and over, I am asked the question How can I find time to do all this reading? My answer? How can I *not* find the time to read? How can I expect our students to find time if I do not? Here are a few tips:

- First, make a pledge to find time each and every day to read. In the summer of 2008, author Laurie Halse Anderson challenged all of her writer friends to join her in a project dubbed WFMAD, Writing Fifteen Minutes a Day. The idea behind this brainchild was to establish a habit. In this case, writing daily was the habit. I accepted the challenge, as I wanted to find some time to continue my work on this book. However, like many educators, I had found excuses, reasons why I could not find the time for writing. So, I joined in the WFMAD challenge. What I discovered was that I *did* manage to find time, even during the most hectic of days, to sit and write. The fifteen-minute requirement was one that I easily surpassed, as it was difficult to stop writing once the ideas began to flow. Most days, I wrote for several hours at a time and even came back a second and third time. The WFMAD pledge made me carve out time each and every day to write. I issue a similar challenge to you, then, as a reader. RFMAD, Reading Fifteen Minutes a Day, is the challenge for you. Find fifteen minutes a day (more is always good) to read a bit from a piece of YA literature. This small commitment can begin to form the habit of finding a regular time to sit and enjoy reading each and every day.

- Use the lists of award winners to narrow down your reading choices from six thousand or so to a more manageable number. It is impossible to read it all, so journey on over to the YALSA website (www.ala.org/yalsa) for list after list of books, including "Great Graphic Novels for Teens," "Teens Top Ten," "Quick Picks for Reluctant Readers," "Best Books for Young Adults," and "Books for the College Bound." Where to begin here depends on your students. If you are trying to light a fire under readers who are less than eager to read, begin with "Quick Picks." If you do not know many graphic novels, begin with that list and work from there. Want to know the books teens love? "Teens Top Ten" is the place to begin.

- Speed up! Faster! Unless we plan to use a novel for an in-depth analysis, we can feel free to read speedily. Read at the pace usually reserved for those lazy summer days.

- Keep notepads or book journals nearby as you read. I tend to keep one of those blank journals with me for jotting down notes and making connections when they occur to me. I know if I do not write something down, it might be forgotten quickly. Develop your own system, though. Naomi Bates, librarian extraordinaire, keeps an Excel spreadsheet with simple information such as title, author, and brief annotation. In the final column, she tries to provide a link to another book.

- Subscribe to reviewing journals if they are not available in your school. *School Library Journal, Booklist, Horn Book, The ALAN Review,* and *VOYA* are a big help as we select new books to include in reading ladders. Many of these journals offer online subscriptions. Remember that other journals often offer review columns, too. Check out *Voices from the Middle, English Journal,* and *The Journal of Adolescent and Adult Literacy.*

- Supplement your reading with audiobooks. During the commute to and from work, while you are running errands or simply working in the garden or around the house, read with your ears. I manage to read dozens more books because I listen to audiobooks (unabridged) as well as read books.

- Relax! Start small, just one or two ladders. Keep up the reading and you will be amazed at how quickly a handful of books become dozens and hundreds and thousands of books.

- Share your knowledge with your colleagues. Start an after-school YA book club. Invite the librarian to be a part of this group (talk about a resource!). Break through the walls of your school and talk to colleagues throughout the district or state. Remember that technology can connect us easily through chat rooms, wikis, and blogs.

Reading ladders can assist us as we strive to motivate our students to read, to read *more*, and to read more widely. This chapter has explored a handful of ways reading ladders could be utilized in your classroom, but that's just the tip of the iceberg. One of the best features of the reading ladder is that it can be adapted, grown, shrunk, stretched, and otherwise altered to fit your students' needs. You're the expert. Start building those ladders!

Climbing the Ladder to Assessment

chapter

7

If you have stayed with me during our many climbs up and down reading ladders, you are aware that there is still one missing piece: assessment. My personal definition of assessment has developed from many years spent working with students who were already being tested entirely too often. I wanted to discover some means of holding students accountable for their reading without giving them yet another test or, quite frankly, annoying them further. Research from more than two decades ago, recently replicated, confirms that many of the assessment strategies and activities we use are counterproductive. That is, they tend to make students *not* want to read. In the 1980s, Mary Livaudais (1986) surveyed students in secondary classrooms in Texas and reported that the traditional book report, whether written or oral, was one of the activities students reported disliking intensely. Her study, replicated by Karen Sue Gibson (2004) and Vicky Giles (2005) in the last ten years, affirmed this finding. In fact, writing letters to characters, writing new chapters for the ending of the book, and creating newspaper articles based on the book—*all* these fairly standard activities were disliked by students. So, how do we hold students accountable?

In part, the answer is that students will tolerate assessments that they believe are worth the time and effort they will put into them. Beyond that, though, students are more willing to complete activities for books they have found worthwhile. Once I moved away from everyone reading the same book at the same time with the same assessment at the end, I found that students were more likely to complete an assessment (and occasionally even be enthusiastic about it). They wanted to let me know what they thought about the book. They also looked forward to letting their peers know about their reading. Of course, there are countless ways to assess students' reading beyond the traditional reporting. Bear in mind, though, that any activity repeated too often will ultimately be numbered among those activities students loathe, so variety is essential. With that in mind, here are some concrete suggestions for assessing student reading.

> In part, the answer is that students will tolerate assessments that they believe are worth the time and effort they will put into them.

Strategies and Activities

Ideas for postreading strategies and activities have been the focus of many professional books and articles. Kylene Beers, Janet Allen, Linda Rief, Harvey Daniels, and Alan Sitomer have covered this territory well in their books and articles. Rather than reinventing the wheel, we can use these strategies and activities as starting points for customizing these tools to our own students' needs, interests, and preferences. Strategies and activities need to be tailored to fit our individual situations.

Over the more than ten years that I was a middle school teacher, I worked with a wide variety of students in different settings. My first position was as a self-contained classroom teacher in an inner-city parochial school. My class was more than 90 percent African American. Compare that with my next teaching job in a public school in the suburbs of Houston, where many of my students were second language learners from Vietnam and Cambodia. While similar activities and strategies worked with each of these distinct sets of students, I needed to make some adjustments to ensure student success. So, take these ideas and make them your own. Tweak, add, and re-create them to meet the needs of your students and classroom.

SIMPLE SIX

Ernest Hemingway once said his greatest short story contained only six words: "For sale: baby shoes, never worn." This incredible feat of wordsmithery is the basis of the idea for this activity. In November 2006, *Smith Magazine* (www.smithmag.net/) teamed with Twitter (twitter.com/; more about Twitter follows in this chapter), asking people to send in six-word memoirs. More than eleven thousand people responded to the challenge. In 2008, Harper Perennial published a book with some of the responses. In 2009, some of the teen responses were published in *I Can't Keep My Own Secrets.* Think of the challenge here! Students could write six-word summaries of books or six-word memoirs of one or more of the characters. The possibilities are endless. Here are a few examples. Note that once again we are beginning with picture books for practice and then moving on to longer works.

- *Where the Wild Things Are*, by Maurice Sendak (1991): Acted badly. Punished. Took amazing journey.
- *The Adventures of Captain Underpants*, by Dav Pilkey (1997): Two boys. One principal. Utter mayhem.
- *Nothing but the Truth*, by Avi (2003): Whole truth? No one tells that.
- *The Graveyard Book*, by Neil Gaiman (2008b): All dead, save one. Ghostly upbringing.
  - Bod: Living in graveyard isn't strange, right?
- *Savvy*, by Ingrid Law (2008): Thirteenth birthday brings changes. Good? Bad?
- *The Nation*, by Terry Pratchett (2008): Tsunami wipes out civilization. Must rebuild.
  - Mau: Lonely. I question my own survival.

I'VE GOT A SECRET

One of the books nominated during my term on the Quick Picks for Reluctant Readers Committee several years ago was *PostSecret*, by Frank Warren (2005). Warren invited people to send him postcards on which they wrote their darkest secrets. The response was more than overwhelming and spawned several books. On each page is a postcard. Some are plain postal cards; others are artistically rendered illustrations. Each contains a secret from the individual who placed it in the mail.

What does this have to do with books and reading and assessment? Ask students to create such a postcard for the protagonist, antagonist, or perhaps their favorite character from the book. What secret would Harry Potter reveal on a postcard from *Harry Potter and the Goblet of Fire* (Rowling 2000)? What postcard would Bella send from

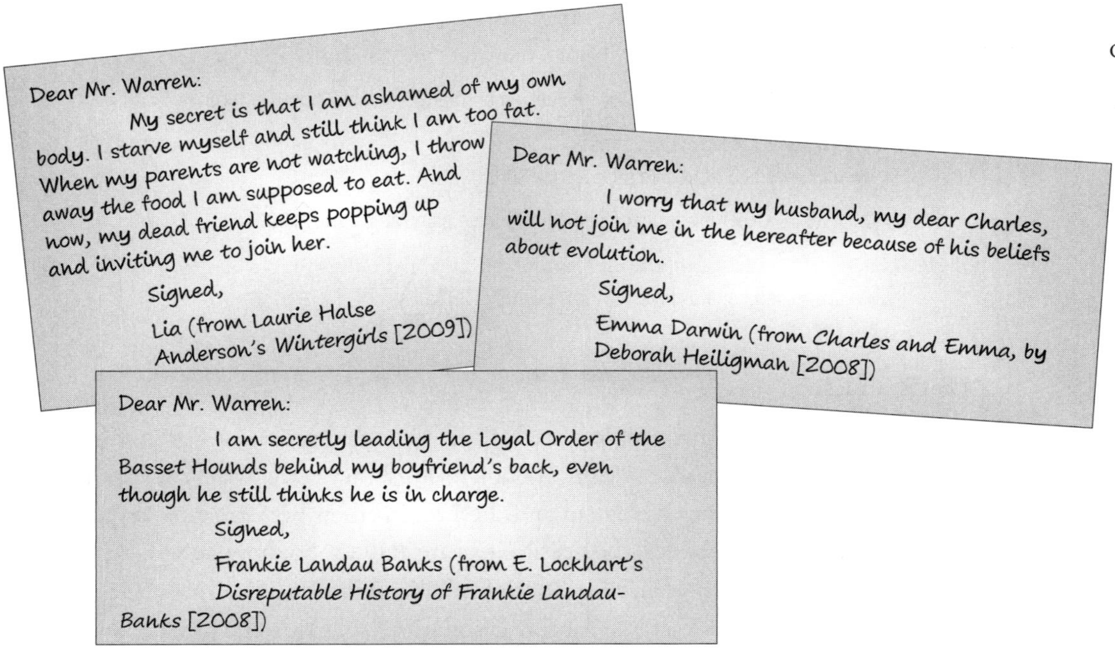

Figure 7.1 *Sample Postcards from Book Characters*

her story, *Twilight* (Meyer 2005)? If students have been reading in literature circles, this activity could replace one of the roles or be done for different characters by various members of the group. The postcards may be plain or include appropriate illustrations. By revealing the darkest secret of the characters, readers demonstrate a deeper knowledge of the book than could be shown by a simple multiple-choice quiz. See if the examples in Figure 7.1 resonate with your students.

ALL ABOARD

Storyboarding is another means to talk about books. Linda Rief discusses the concept of storyboarding as a prewriting, drafting, and revising tool. I think this same technique works well for summarizing a plot or detailing character development. Storyboarding transforms words into images. However, students do not need to be accomplished artists to prepare and present a storyboard. Illustrations can be simple (stick figures and the like), or students can use computer graphics or illustrations from other sources. A terrific resource is the comic strip *Unshelved*. During the week, this strip features the antics of a group of public librarians, but on Sundays, the comic manages to tell the story behind one book, ranging from adults' to children's.

For more information, and to see sample strips, visit this URL: www.unshelved .com/. Here are some links to YA books featured in Sunday strips:

Audrey, Wait! (Benway 2008) www.unshelved.com/archive.aspx?strip=20080824

Adventures in Oz: (Shanower 2006)
     www.unshelved.com/archive.aspx?strip=20080803

Slam: (Hornby 2007) www.unshelved.com/archive.aspx?strip=20071007

Alcatraz Versus the Evil Librarians: (Sanderson 2007)
     www.unshelved.com/archive.aspx?strip=20071202

Hear Here

Podcasts make possible some simple but effective assessment activities. For instance, you could have students make podcasts of book reviews; they could write readers theatre scripts from books they have read and then record their performances as podcasts. Once you have the basics, the possibilities are endless. So, how do you begin?

The first logical step is to write a script of what will be said during the podcast. (Of course, if the podcast will capture a literature circle or some other less formal format, you won't need a script.) Once the script is completed and rehearsed, recording can begin. With headphones and a microphone, the recording can be done directly into a program on the computer. Digital voice recorders can also be used. Adding sound effects can add to the depth of the recording.

A few years ago, I decided to record the booktalking sessions I was conducting in schools. I added a mike to my iPod (an attachment that is relatively inexpensive and simply allows you to record using the iPod). After the recording was completed, I transferred the audio file into editing software (I use Audacity, since it is free) and created a podcast to upload to my blog. Teachers and librarians could then listen to the podcast and design ones of their own. The entire process from start to finish took only a few hours of my time.

A handy resource for teachers wanting to explore the use of podcasts with students is Kristin Fontichiaro's *Podcasting at School* (2008). The Web has many podcasts of booktalks you and your students might use as models. Nancy Keane posts a short podcast on a new book each day at her website: www.nancykeane.com/.

Down the Tube

Videos, known as book trailers, constitute another step up the ladder, so to speak. Book trailers have become the new hot way to promote books. These videos can be full-fledged booktalks or simply short teasers designed to make someone else want to read the book—an ad, if you will. YouTube has tons of examples of book trailers, from those done professionally to those completed by fans of the books.

Some simple directions can be found at Naomi Bates' blog (naomibates .blogspot.com/). Naomi is a former student of mine and an enthusiastic high school librarian who advocates YA literature to her students and staff. She makes the following suggestions for making book trailers. Bear in mind that creating videos is a logical extension of storyboarding.

1. Use Photo Story or Movie Maker. These programs are quite user-friendly, but you can generally locate information and training online or at professional meetings. Some of these programs are free (Photo Story); others may need to be purchased. Programs are available for both PC and Mac platforms.

2. Be certain to select a book that somehow unfolds as a video as you are reading it.

3. Brainstorm a list of words or phrases associated with the book, the characters, the setting, the conflict. Are there colors that are important to the story, either literally or figuratively? Is there one image that is central to the book? Compile these lists.

4. Begin searching for images from online sources. There are many online resources, such as the Library of Congress and Wikimedia. Clip art files that come with bundled computer programs are another source, as are photos from home files. Be certain that complete attribution is noted for any images collected.

5. Upload the images and begin placing them in some sort of order. Write captions for the images as you place them on individual slides. This is a preliminary draft, so nothing is set in cement yet.

6. Revision is next. Time to fine-tune the order of slides and the captions. Also begin thinking about colors and fonts and images that hang together and create some visual unity. Effects, transitions, color, and timing are at issue in this phase.

7. Consider adding music or sound effects at this juncture. It is best if there is *one* piece that underlies the entire video for consistency; however, there may be times when mood changes dictate music changes.

Here are some links for video book trailers:

Boys That Bite: www.youtube.com/watch?v=TWvqWCcB4_I

Airman: www.youtube.com/watch?v=QSdDYjhuywQ

Deadline: www.youtube.com/watch?v=jcY9WXPXVdA

Gone: www.youtube.com/watch?v=uf8B3FM1L8c

Love, Stargirl: www.youtube.com/watch?v=tMoXMhqI0L0&feature=related

Booktrailers4all

http://www.teachertube.com/viewProfile.php?user=Booktrailers4all Another of my former students, Teresa Schauer, began using TeacherTube so that teachers and librarians could share book trailers. YouTube is often filtered by school firewalls. TeacherTube trailers should be accessible.

A BOOK MEME

Memes (rhymes with *themes*) originated with the work of Richard Dawkins, who coined the word as a neologism to describe melodies, catchphrases, beliefs, clothing and fashion, and other cultural aspects. The Internet has taken hold of the meme concept and used it in social networking situations to encourage people to reveal more about themselves. So, how does this relate to assessment?

Memes can be a format for nontraditional book reports. Consider the following questions:

1. Which book is the first one you read that touched you in some deep way?

2. What book did everyone else like and you hated?

3. Do you flip to the last page and read it first or do you force yourself to wait until the end?

4. Which book character would you switch places with?

5. Do you have a book that reminds you of something specific in your life (a person, a place, a time)?

6. What is the strangest item you've ever found in a book?

7. Have you ever seen a movie you liked better than the book?

8. Conversely, which book should *never* have been made into a movie?

9. Who is the person whose book advice you'll always take?

10. What is the worst book you have ever read?

This meme will help you get to know your students better. Be certain to share your own answers to these questions, too. We can also use the concept of a meme for assessment of reading. Figure 7.2 contains a few questions that students could use to discuss the characters in the books they read. Students should select five or six of the questions and answer them as one of the characters in their book. Certainly, this is just the beginning. You can come up with additional questions and even ask students to brainstorm along with you.

CHARACTER MEME QUESTIONS

1. What is the best book you ever read?

2. Last page: read it first or wait until the end?

3. Do you have a book that reminds you of something specific in your life (a person, a place, a time)?

4. Any required reading you hated in high school?

5. What is the strangest item you've ever found in a book?

6. Do you purchase used or brand-new books?

7. Have you ever seen a movie you liked better than the book?

8. Conversely, which book should *never* have been introduced to film?

9. Who is the person whose advice you'll always take?

10. If you could trade places with any other person in this book, who would it be?

Figure 7.2 *Character Meme Questions*

KISS

"Keep it simple, stupid" is a mantra I come back to again and again. Anything I assign for students to complete is, in turn, something I will have to grade by the hundreds later. So, I try to formulate activities that are relatively quick and painless for me to assess. Once I have developed my own activity or tweaked someone else's, I practice it with classes of students. Ultimately, they are free to select from a variety of assessment activities themselves.

Create some of these generic assessments; brainstorm a list of questions that could be the focus for fiction or informational books; develop more roles for literature circle participants. And don't forget to use ladders, as well. Finally, consider using picture books as you introduce these alternatives to the more traditional forms of assessment. Picture books, because of their brevity, offer us the chance to demonstrate and model for our students the products we expect. Figure 7.3 contains a list of picture books that work well with older readers.

Using shorter pieces of literature can not only help us offer instruction but also assist us in turning the decisions about assessment over to the students. We can provide students with many different strategies and activities for assessment, give them practice in those strategies and activities, and then allow them to select which to use to assess their understanding after reading.

PICTURE BOOKS FOR OLDER READERS

Black and White by David Macaulay (1990)

Multiple points of view eventually combine to create one coherent narrative. Point of view is one element that can be taught using this unique picture book.

Bubba and Beau Meet the Relatives by Kathi Appelt (2004)

Dialect plays an essential role in this story with a Texas twang. Think about this one when teaching dialect, voice, word choice, and other elements of good writing.

Chato and the Party Animals by Gary Soto (2000)

Analyzing the use of color to convey mood is one way to utilize this picture book with a Spanish flavor.

Click Clack Moo: Cows That Type by Doreen Cronin (2000)

Clear and concise correspondence might be one focus for a lesson using this book, the first in a series featuring Farmer Brown and his animal menagerie.

Flossie and the Fox by Patricia McKissack (1986)

This is one variant of the story of Little Red Riding Hood. Combine several of these stories and use them to work on classificatory writing and thinking.

Hey, Al by Arthur Yorinks (1986)

Introducing readers to classic themes is simple with picture books such as this one, which explores similar territory to "The Monkey's Paw," by W. W. Jacobs.

Jumanji by Chris Van Allsburg (1981)

Forget the movie and examine this black-and-white picture book whose illustrations use perspective to focus readers' attention.

Lotus Seed by Sherry Garland (1993)

Picture books can be used to infuse more multicultural literature into the curriculum. This story of Vietnamese immigrants is just one example.

Mufaro's Beautiful Daughters by John Steptoe (1987)

An African variant of the Cinderella story, this exquisitely illustrated picture book employs symbolism both visually and textually.

Officer Buckle and Gloria by Peggy Rathmann (1995)

The disconnect between illustration and story can be helpful in developing visual literacy.

Olivia by Ian Falconer (2000)

Black and white and red are the sole colors in this humorous picture book. Use it to work on understanding symbolism.

Patrol by Walter Dean Myers (2001)

This picture book explores the complex issues of war. Think of pairing it with Hemingway's *Farewell to Arms* (1986), *Soldier's Heart* (Paulsen 1998), and other longer works.

Rose Blanche by Roberto Innocenti (1996)

Winner of a Batchelder Award, this picture book focuses on World War II and the Nazi occupation of countries. Not only a terrific content area tie-in, this book also demonstrates the powerful use of point of view.

Smoky Night by Eve Bunting (1994)

Realia (actual objects) art can assist in teaching symbolism. Point of view is also essential in this look at riots from a child's perspective.

Sophie by Mem Fox (1994)

Simple language speaks volumes about the circle of life and intergenerational relationships.

The Talking Eggs by Robert San Souci (1989)

Here is another Cinderella variant, this one from the American South.

Three Pigs by David Wiesner (2001)

This fairy tale variant is perfect for a discussion of setting, character development, and climax.

Three Questions by Jon Muth (2002)

This philosophical story, based on the writing of Leo Tolstoy, offers examples of metaphor, fable, and allegory.

Tops and Bottoms by Janet Stevens (1995)

While illustrations could certainly be one focus of this Caldecott-winning picture book, the story could set the stage for "The Ransom of Red Chief" and other stories by O. Henry.

Where the Wild Things Are by Maurice Sendak (1991)

Teaching theme is simplified with this classic Caldecott-winning title.

Figure 7.3 *Picture Books for Older Readers*

TWEET TWEET!

The advent of different social networking sites and tools can also provide us with some interesting ways to talk about books after reading. Twitter (twitter.com/), with its limit of 140 characters per posting (tweet), is one way to encourage brevity when discussing various components of books. Teachers could set up a twibe, a closed community, of students and ask students to post short thoughts about character analysis, symbolism, plot events, and more. If your school filters Twitter, and chances are it does, you can still set up a discussion board where students are limited to 140-character postings. Different groups may be set up for different books. Or, if students are all reading individual books, the common thread for the group may simply be a teacher prompt. You might consider using one of the meme questions as a prompt. If you have access to a system that permits voice threads, these postings may be done orally instead of in writing.

> Twitter (twitter.com/), with its limit of 140 characters per posting (tweet), is one way to encourage brevity when discussing various components of books.

Lincoln Logs Redux

Readers are built, one book at a time. Recently, someone suggested that we assign students the task of creating a reading time line. Along the line, students would note the books and people and events that helped shape them as the readers they are at this moment. This is similar to the reading autobiography I penned when I took my YA literature class from Dick Abrahamson almost twenty years ago. The reading autobiography is a narrative. The reading time line presents similar information in a different format. A portion of my reading time line might look like this:

1953—Grandfather reads aloud *Pat the Bunny*.

1955—I learn to read on my own using *Put Me in the Circus* and *Hop on Pop*.

1957—Basal readers—Who cares about Dick and Jane and Spot?

1962—Forced to read *Great Expectations*. Do not like it. Do not finish it.

1963—Christmas means the entire set of Nancy Drew!

1966—"A Member of the Wedding" is my favorite story of all time this year.

1967–70—Read only what is required and do not care much for any of it.

1977—Read first YA novel and fell in love.

I wonder what your reading time line would look like? Could we perhaps create a *huge* time line that ran around the classroom and ask each student to place important books and events and people along it? Imagine a class reading time line and the discussion it could generate. Mostly, I hope it would absolutely underscore the fact that many of us take different paths to get to a lifetime of reading. It should also underscore, though, that we share some commonalities. What are those? After students post the books and experiences and events and influences along the time line, take time to analyze those similarities. I suspect they will include elements from the following list. These elements should guide us in our teaching and in our sharing of our own reading with our students.

1. Providing satisfying reading experiences for our students through reading aloud and booktalking.

2. Providing access to books through classroom, school, and public libraries.

3. Providing alternative media: audiobooks and ebooks, for instance.

4. Providing slow and careful progression from one book to another and another.

5. And most importantly, providing students a model through our own reading.

If we provide satisfying reading experiences through reading aloud and booktalks, access through libraries of all kinds, alternative ways to read, ladders that gently move students between books, and leadership through example, we have begun the work of building readers with a solid foundation.

Remember the building blocks we discussed in Chapter 2: reading aloud, access to books, and models of literacy. These are those first Lincoln Logs that build the foundation for lifetime readers and lifelong learners. We build on that foundation by allowing time during the school day for free reading, reading for pleasure. We increase its strength by ensuring that students are permitted to linger over a favorite book or genre or author before moving on or even that they are permitted to read backward and return to an old favorite later (I still enjoy time spent rereading *Charlotte's Web*). We build up more from that foundation with the creation of reading ladders that mirror the interests and preferences of our students. We provide strong materials through our own reading of YA literature. We add stories onto our foundation, slowly creating strong and independent readers.

But we need to take care. Lincoln Logs may topple unless we build carefully. So it is with readers. We need to be patient and add experiences as students are ready so that the solid foundation can support the building. Just think of readers who continue to grow and grow and become lifelong readers; they take that foundation and create of themselves veritable skyscrapers, buildings that soar into the heavens and aspire to rise above everything. All right, enough hyperbole. We have come to the final stage of our building project. We now have an external structure to support our students. Now, we need to begin the work on the remainder of

We need to be patient and add experiences as students are ready so that the solid foundation can support the building.

the structure. Paint, drywall, floors, doorways, ceilings, windows, and the like are still to be added. How does all this happen? If we have done the work of laying a good foundation, our students should be able to design the rest of the structure throughout their lifetimes.

In the last month of working on this book, I pledged to read a book a day for a month. Some books were floors: they helped me gain some footing on an issue or topic. Kelly Gallagher's *Readicide* was one of those books. Other books were paint and wallpaper: they were colorful and added depth to my reading. For instance, I read tons of new picture books, books that required I read words and pictures. Audiobooks were doorways, particularly as I listened to books I had already read, such as *Coraline*, by Neil Gaiman. Reading with my ears opened some new doors into my understanding of this gothic novel. And the windows? Nearly every YA book I read that month permitted me a window not only to the lives of teens but to my own life as well.

In Langston Hughes' poem "Mother to Son," a mother exhorts her child to keep climbing the stairs. Even at her age, she cries, she is still climbing even though the climbing is not easy. I think we need to heed this advice: to keep reading, to keep climbing, to keep exhorting our students to come along with us.

Trade Book Bibiolography

What follows is a list of all of the various children's and YA books mentioned throughout this book. These are the books included in the reading ladders and in other discussions within the chapters. While it is a good place to begin, please keep in mind that these books are intended for a wide range of ages and interests. It is a good starting point, though, for your reading and for beginning the construction of those first reading ladders. Online resources are invaluable to me when searching for books and bibliographic information. Amazon (www.amazon.com/) is one option for finding information. Titlewave (www.titlewave.com/) is another, and anyone can open a free Titlewave account which gives you access to not only bibliographic information but full-text reviews of books and reading levels and Lexiles if these are items you need as well.

Abadzis, N. 2007. *Laika*. New York: First Second.

Abel, J., and G. Soria. 2007. *Life Sucks*. New York: First Second.

Almond, D. 2008. *The Savage*. Cambridge, MA: Candlewick.

Anderson, L. H. 2000a. *Fever, 1793*. New York: Simon and Schuster Books for Young Readers.

———. 2000b. *Speak*. Carmel, CA: Hampton-Brown.

———. 2005. *Prom*. New York: Viking.

———. 2007. *Twisted*. New York: Viking.

———. 2009. *Wintergirls*. New York: Viking.

Anderson, M. T. 2002. *Feed*. Cambridge, MA: Candlewick.

Appelt, K. 2004. *Bubba and Beau Meet the Relatives*. Orlando: Harcourt.

———. 2008. *The Underneath*. New York: Atheneum Books for Young Readers.

Avi. 2003. *Nothing but the Truth: A Documentary Novel*. New York: Orchard Books.

———. 2008. *Acting Out*. New York: Atheneum.

Bang, M. 1991. *Picture This! Perception and Composition*. Boston: Little, Brown.

Bartoletti, S. C. 2005. *Hitler Youth: Growing Up in Hitler's Shadow*. New York: Scholastic Nonfiction.

————. 2008. *The Boy Who Dared*. New York: Scholastic.

Bauer, J. 2008. *Peeled*. New York: G. P. Putnam's Sons.

Bennett, J. 1982. *The Executioner*. New York: Avon Books.

Benway, R. 2008. *Audrey, Wait!* New York: Razorbill.

Black, H. 2004. *Tithe: A Modern Faerie Tale*. New York: Simon Pulse.

————. 2006. *Valiant: A Modern Tale of Faerie*. Waterville, ME: Thorndike.

————. 2008. *Kin*. The Good Neighbors Book 1. New York: Graphix.

Blackwood, G. 2005. *Second Sight*. New York: Dutton Children's Books.

Bloor, E. 2006. *London Calling*. New York: Alfred A. Knopf.

Bodeen, S. A. 2008. *The Compound*. New York: Feiwel and Friends.

Bosch, P. 2007. *The Name of This Book Is Secret*. New York: Little, Brown.

Boyne, J. 2006. *The Boy in the Striped Pajamas: A Fable*. Oxford; New York: David Fickling Books.

Bray, L. 2007. *The Sweet Far Thing*. New York: Delacorte.

Broach, E. 2008. *Masterpiece*. New York: Henry Holt.

Brooks, K. 2008. *Black Rabbit Summer*. New York: Scholastic.

Bunting, E. 1994. *Smoky Night*. San Diego: Harcourt Brace.

Burg, S. 2008. *A Thousand Never Ends*. New York: Delacorte.

Butzer, C. M. 2009. *Gettysburg: The Graphic Novel*. New York: Bowen.

Carle, E. 1998. *Hello, Red Fox*. New York: Simon and Schuster Books for Young Readers.

Cart, M., comp. 1999. *Tomorrowland: Ten Stories About the Future*. New York: Scholastic.

Castellucci, C. 2007. *The Plain Janes*. New York: Minx.

Clare, C. 2007. *City of Bones*. New York: M. K. McElderry Books.

Cohn, R., and D. Levithan. 2006. *Nick and Norah's Infinite Playlist*. New York: Knopf.

Colfer, E., and A. Donkin. 2007. *Artemis Fowl: The Graphic Novel*. New York: Hyperion Books for Children.

Collins, S. 2008. *The Hunger Games*. New York: Scholastic.

Cormier, R. 1997. *Tenderness: A Novel*. New York: Delacorte.

————. 2004. *The Chocolate War*. 30th ann. ed. New York: Knopf.

Corrigan, E. 2004. *Splintering*. New York: Scholastic.

Cottrell Boyce, F. 2004. *Millions*. New York: HarperCollins.

Couloumbis, A. 2008. *Love Me Tender*. New York: Random House.

Cover, A. B. 2005. *William Shakespeare's Macbeth: The Graphic Novel*. New York: Puffin Books.

Coville, B. 2008. "The Mask of Eamonn Tiyado." In *Oddest of All: Stories*. Orlando: Harcourt.

Crane, S. 2005. *The Red Badge of Courage*. West Berlin, NJ: Townsend.

Creech, S. 1994. *Walk Two Moons*. New York: HarperCollins.

————. 2001. *Love That Dog.* New York: HarperCollins.

————. 2008. *Hate That Cat.* New York: Joanna Cotler Books.

Cronin, D. 2000. *Click, Clack, Moo: Cows That Type.* New York: Simon and Schuster Books for Young Readers.

Crowe, C. 2002. *Mississippi Trial, 1955.* New York: Phyllis Fogelman Books.

————. 2003. *Getting Away with Murder: The True Story of the Emmett Till Case.* New York: Phyllis Fogelman Books.

————. 2004. *More than a Game: Sports Literature for Young Adults.* Lanham, MD: Scarecrow.

Crutcher, C. 1991. *Athletic Shorts: Six Short Stories.* New York: Greenwillow Books.

————. 2003. *King of the Mild Frontier.* New York: Greenwillow Books.

————. 2007. *Deadline.* New York: Greenwillow Books.

Curtis, C. P. 1995. *The Watsons Go to Birmingham—1963: A Novel.* New York: Delacorte.

————. 2004. *Bucking the Sarge.* New York: Wendy Lamb Books.

————. 2007a. *Elijah of Buxton.* New York: Scholastic.

————. 2007b. *Mr. Chickee's Messy Mission.* New York: Random House Children's Books.

————. 2008. *Elijah of Buxton.* Audiobook. Narr. M. Willis. New York: Listening Library.

Dahl, R. 2002. *Roald Dahl's Revolting Rhymes.* Rev. ed. New York: Knopf.

Danziger, P., and A. M. Martin. 1998. *P.S. Longer Letter Later.* New York: Scholastic.

————. 2000. *Snail Mail No More.* New York: Scholastic.

dePaola, T. 1983. *Legend of the Bluebonnet: An Old Tale of Texas.* New York: Putnam.

Deuker, C. 1993. *Heart of a Champion: A Novel.* New York: Little, Brown.

————. 2007a. *Gym Candy.* Boston: Houghton Mifflin.

————. 2007b. *Runner.* Boston: Houghton Mifflin.

DiCamillo, K. 2003. *The Tale of Despereaux: Being the Story of a Mouse, a Princess, Some Soup, and a Spool of Thread.* Cambridge, MA: Candlewick.

Dickinson, P. 1989. *Eva.* New York: Delacorte.

Doctorow, C. 2008. *Little Brother.* New York: Tor Teen.

Donnelly, J. 2003. *A Northern Light.* San Diego: Harcourt.

Dowd, S. 2008. *The London Eye Mystery.* Oxford; New York: David Fickling Books.

Downham, J. 2007. *Before I Die.* New York: David Fickling Books.

Draper, S. M. 2001. *Romiette and Julio.* New York: Simon Pulse.

Dunkle, C. B. 2008. *The Sky Inside.* New York: Atheneum Books for Young Readers.

Dunn, M. 2001. *Ella Minnow Pea: A Novel in Letters.* New York: Anchor Books.

Ellis, A. D. 2009. *Everything Is Fine.* New York: Little, Brown.

Engle, M. 2008. *The Surrender Tree: Poems of Cuba's Struggle for Freedom.* New York: Henry Holt.

Falconer, I. 2000. *Olivia.* New York: Atheneum Books for Young Readers.

Fleischman, P. 1993. *Bull Run*. New York: HarperCollins.

————. 2004. *Seedfolks*. New York: HarperTrophy.

Fox, M. 1994. *Sophie*. San Diego: Harcourt Brace.

Frost, R. 2001. *Stopping by Woods on a Snowy Evening*. New York: Dutton.

Gaiman, N. 2002. *Coraline*. New York: HarperCollins.

————. 2007. *M Is for Magic*. New York: HarperCollins.

————. 2008a. *Coraline*. Graphic novel. New York: HarperCollins.

————. 2008b. *The Graveyard Book*. New York: HarperCollins.

Gallo, D. R., ed. 1990. *Center Stage: One-Act Plays for Teenage Readers and Actors*. New York: Harper and Row.

————. 1992. *Short Circuits: Thirteen Shocking Stories by Outstanding Writers for Young Adults*. New York: Delacorte.

Gantos, J. 1997. *Jack's New Power: Stories from a Caribbean Year*. New York: Farrar, Straus and Giroux.

————. 1999. *Jack on the Tracks: Four Seasons of Fifth Grade*. New York: Farrar, Straus and Giroux.

————. 2002. *A Hole in My Life*. New York: Farrar, Straus and Giroux.

————. 2005. *Jack's Black Book*. New York: Farrar, Straus and Giroux.

Garfinkle, D. L. 2008. *Fowl Language*. Supernatural Rubber Chicken Book 1. Renton, WA: Mirrorstone.

Garland, S. 1993. *Lotus Seed*. San Diego: Harcourt Brace Jovanovich.

Gee, J. 2007. *Encyclopedia Horrifica: The Terrifying Truth About Vampires, Ghosts, Monsters, and More*. New York: Scholastic.

Gerstein, M. 2003. *The Man Who Walked Between the Towers*. Brookfield, CT: Roaring Brook.

Giff, P. R. 2002. *Pictures of Hollis Woods*. New York: Wendy Lamb Books.

Gill, D. M. 2009. *Soul Enchilada*. New York: Greenwillow Books.

Gipi. 2007. *Garage Band*. New York: First Second.

Glenn, M. 1982. *Class Dismissed! High School Poems*. New York: Clarion Books.

————. 1997. *The Taking of Room 114: A Hostage Drama in Poems*. New York: Lodestar Books.

————. 1999. *Foreign Exchange: A Mystery in Poems*. New York: Morrow Junior Books.

Grandits, J. 2004. *Technically, It's Not My Fault: Concrete Poems*. New York: Clarion Books.

————. 2007. *Blue Lipstick: Concrete Poems*. New York: Clarion Books.

Gray, C. 2008. *Evernight*. New York: HarperTeen.

Green, J. 2005. *Looking for Alaska*. New York: Dutton Children's Books.

————. 2008. *Paper Towns*. New York: Dutton Books.

Gregerson, J. 2007. *Bad Girls Club*. Austin, TX: Blooming Tree.

Griffith, S. 2007. *Howtoons: The Possibilities Are Endless!* New York: Collins.

Griffiths, A. 2008. *What Buttosaur Is That?* New York: Scholastic Paperbacks.

Guinness World Records Limited. 2009. *Guinness World Records 2009*. New York: Bantam Dell.

Haddix, M. P. 2008. *Found*. New York: Simon and Schuster Books for Young Readers.

Hale, B. 2003. *The Malted Falcon: From the Tattered Casebook of Chet Gecko, Private Eye*. San Diego: Harcourt.

———. 2004. *Murder, My Tweet: From the Tattered Casebook of Chet Gecko, Private Eye*. Orlando: Harcourt.

Hale, S. 2008. *Rapunzel's Revenge*. New York: Bloomsbury.

Hawthorne, N. 2009. *The Scarlet Letter*. San Francisco: Ignatius.

Headley, J. C. 2009. *North of Beautiful*. New York: Little, Brown.

Heiligman, D. 2009. *Charles and Emma: The Darwins' Leap of Faith*. New York: Henry Holt.

Helfer, A. 2006. *Malcolm X: A Graphic Biography*. New York: Hill and Wang.

Hemingway, E. 1986. *A Farewell to Arms*. New York: Collier Books.

Hemphill, H. 2007. *Runaround*. Asheville, NC: Front Street.

Henkes, K. 2003. *Olive's Ocean*. New York: Greenwillow Books.

Hennessey, J. 2008. *The United States Constitution: A Graphic Adaptation*. New York: Hill and Wang.

Hesse, K. 1995. *Phoenix Rising*. New York: Puffin Books.

———. 1997. *Out of the Dust*. New York: Scholastic.

———. 1998. *The Music of Dolphins*. New York: Scholastic.

———. 2001. *Witness*. New York: Scholastic.

Hiaasen, C. 2009. *Scat*. New York: Alfred A. Knopf.

Hill, L. C. 2007. *America Dreaming*. New York: Little, Brown.

Hinds, G. 2007. *Beowulf*. Cambridge, MA: Candlewick.

———. 2008. *The Merchant of Venice: A Play*. Cambridge, MA: Candlewick.

Hinton, S. E. 1967. *The Outsiders*. New York: Viking.

Holm, J. L., and M. Holm. 2005. *BabyMouse*. New York: Random House Children's Books.

Holman, F. 1986. *Slake's Limbo*. New York: Aladdin Books.

Hopkins, E. 2007. *Glass*. New York: Margaret K. McElderry Books.

———. 2008. *Identical*. New York: Margaret K. McElderry Books.

Hornby, N. 2007. *Slam*. New York: Putnam.

Horvath, P. 2001. *Everything on a Waffle*. New York: Farrar, Straus and Giroux.

———. 2005. *The Canning Season*. New York: Farrar, Straus and Giroux.

———. 2007. *The Corps of the Bare-Boned Plane*. New York: Farrar, Straus and Giroux.

———. 2008. *My One Hundred Adventures*. New York: Schwartz and Wade Books.

Hurley, T. 2008. *Ghostgirl*. Boston: Little, Brown.

Huxley, A. 1989. *Brave New World*. New York: Harper and Row.

Innocenti, R. 1996. *Rose Blanche*. San Diego: Creative Editions/Harcourt Brace.

Jacobson, S., and E. Colon. 2006. *The 9/11 Report: A Graphic Adaptation*. New York: Hill and Wang.

Jacques, B. 2007. *Redwall: The Graphic Novel*. New York: Philomel Books.

Jenkins, A. M. 2008. *Night Road*. New York: HarperTeen.

Jocelyn, M. 2008. *Would You*. New York: Wendy Lamb Books.

Juster, N. 1996. *The Phantom Tollbooth*. New York: Random House.

Kehret, P. 1991. *Acting Natural: Monologs, Dialogs, and Playlets for Teens*. Colorado Springs: Meriwether.

Ketteman, H. 1997. *Bubba the Cowboy Prince: A Fractured Texas Tale*. New York: Scholastic.

Kibuishi, K. 2008. *The Stonekeeper*. Amulet Book 1. New York: Graphix.

Kinney, J. 2007. *Diary of a Wimpy Kid*. New York: Amulet Books.

Klass, D. 2002. *You Don't Know Me: A Novel*. New York: HarperTempest.

Klise, K. 2006. *Regarding the Bathroom: A Privy to the Past*. Orlando: Harcourt.

Korman, G. 1989. "A Reasonable Sum." In *Connections: Short Stories by Outstanding Writers for Young Adults*, ed. D. R. Gallo. New York: Delacorte.

Kunhardt, D. M. 1940. *Pat the Bunny*. New York: Simon and Schuster.

Kuper, P. 2003. *The Metamorphosis*. New York: Crown.

Lanagan, M. 2005. *Black Juice*. New York: Eos.

Landy, D. 2007. *Skulduggery Pleasant*. New York: HarperCollins.

Larbalestier, J. 2008. *How to Ditch Your Fairy*. New York: Bloomsbury Children's Books.

Larson, K. 2006. *Hattie Big Sky*. New York: Delacorte.

Law, I. 2008. *Savvy*. New York; Boston: Dial Books for Young Readers; Walton Media.

Leedy, L. 2003. *There's a Frog in My Throat! 440 Animal Sayings a Little Bird Told Me*. New York: Holiday House.

———. 2008. *Crazy Like a Fox: A Simile Story*. New York: Holiday House.

Levine, G. C. 2007. *Fairest*. Audiobook. Narr. S. Naughton. Syracuse, NY: Full Cast Audio.

Levithan, D. 2006. *The Realm of Possibility*. New York: Knopf.

Lockhart, E. 2008. *The Disreputable History of Frankie Landau-Banks: A Novel*. New York: Hyperion.

Lowry, L. 2002. *The Giver*. St. Paul, MN: EMC/Paradigm.

———. 2008. *The Willoughbys*. Boston: Houghton Mifflin.

Lubar, D. 2007. *True Talents*. New York: Tom Doherty.

Lutes, J. 2007. *Houdini: The Handcuff King*. New York: Hyperion.

Lynch, C. 2006. *Sins of the Fathers*. New York: HarperTempest.

Macaulay, D. 1988. *The Way Things Work*. Boston: Houghton Mifflin.

————. 1990. *Black and White*. Boston: Houghton Mifflin.

Mackler, C. 2003. *The Earth, My Butt, and Other Big Round Things*. Cambridge, MA: Candlewick.

Martin, A. M., and R. Telgemeier. 2006. *Kristy's Great Idea; A Graphic Novel*. The Baby-Sitters Club Graphic Novel 1. New York: Graphix.

McKissack, P. 1986. *Flossie and the Fox*. New York: Dial Books for Young Readers.

Mead, R. 2007. *Vampire Academy*. New York: Razorbill.

Meldrum, C. 2008. *Madapple*. New York: Alfred A. Knopf.

Meyer, L. A. 2008. *Curse of the Blue Tattoo*. Bloody Jack Book 2. Audiobook. Narr. K. Kellgren. Roseland, NJ: Listen and Live Audio.

Meyer, S. 2005. *Twilight*. New York: Little, Brown.

————. 2006. *New Moon*. New York: Little, Brown.

————. 2008a. *Breaking Dawn*. New York: Little, Brown.

————. 2008b. *Eclipse*. New York: Little, Brown.

Miéville, C. 2008. *Un Lun Dun*. New York: Del Rey.

Morse, S. 2008. *Magic Pickle*. New York: Graphix.

Murdock, C. G. 2006. *Dairy Queen: A Novel*. Boston: Houghton Mifflin.

————. 2007. *The Off Season*. Boston: Houghton Mifflin.

Murrie, S., and M. Murrie. 2007. *Every Minute on Earth: Fun Facts That Happen Every 60 Seconds*. New York: Scholastic Reference.

Muth, J. J. 2002. *The Three Questions*. New York: Scholastic.

Myers, W. D. 2001. *Patrol: An American Soldier in Vietnam*. New York: HarperCollins.

————. 2008a. *Jazz*. Audiobook. Narr. J. Williams and V. Thomas. Pine Plains, NY: Live Oak Media.

————. 2008b. *Sunrise over Fallujah*. New York: Scholastic.

Myracle, L. 2004. *Ttyl*. New York: Amulet Books.

————. 2006. *Ttfn*. New York: Amulet Books.

————. 2007. *L8r, G8r*. New York: Amulet Books.

Naylor, P. R. 1991. *Shiloh*. New York; Toronto: Atheneum; Collier Macmillan Canada.

Nelson, K. 2008. *We Are the Ship: The Story of Negro League Baseball*. New York: Jump at the Sun/Hyperion Books for Children.

Nickel, S. 2006. *Night of the Homework Zombies*. Mankato, MN: Stone Arch Books.

Nixon, J. L. 1991. *Whispers from the Dead*. New York: Laurel-Leaf.

Nolan, H. 2006. *A Summer of Kings*. Orlando: Harcourt.

O'Connor, B. 2007. *How to Steal a Dog*. New York: Farrar, Straus and Giroux.

O'Neill, M. L. D. 1989. *Hailstones and Halibut Bones: Adventures in Color*. New York: Doubleday.

Orwell, G. 2007. *1984*. Jackson Hole, WY: Archeion.

Palatini, M. 2008. *Geek Chic: The Zoey Zone*. New York: HarperCollins Children's Books.

Paterson, K. 2007. *Bridge to Terabithia*. New York: HarperEntertainment.

Patterson, J. 2007. *Maximum Ride: Saving the World and Other Extreme Sports*. New York: Little, Brown.

Paulsen, G. 1993. *Nightjohn*. Audiobook. Narr. M.-D. Woods. Prince Frederick, MD: Recorded Books.

———. 1997. *The Schernoff Discoveries*. New York: Delacorte.

———. 1998. *Soldier's Heart: A Novel of the Civil War*. New York: Delacorte.

———. 2007. *Harris and Me: A Summer Remembered*. Orlando: Harcourt.

Pearson, M. 2008. *The Adoration of Jenna Fox*. New York: Henry Holt.

Peck, R. 1984. "Priscilla and the Wimps." In *Sixteen: Short Stories by Outstanding Writers for Young Adults*, ed. D. Gallo. New York: Delacorte.

———. 2007. *On the Wings of Heroes*. New York: Dial Books.

Perel, D., and the editors of the *Weekly World News*. 2005. *Bat Boy Lives! The Weekly World News Guide to Politics, Culture, Celebrities, Alien Abductions, and the Mutant Freaks That Shape Our World*. New York: Sterling.

Perez, M. 2008. *Dead Is the New Black*. Orlando: Harcourt.

Pfeffer, S. B. 2006. *Life as We Knew It*. Orlando: Harcourt.

———. 2008. *The Dead and the Gone*. Orlando: Harcourt.

Philbrick, R. 1999. "The Last Book in the Universe." In *Tomorrowland: Ten Stories About the Future*. Comp. M. Cart. New York: Scholastic.

———. 2000. *The Last Book in the Universe*. New York: Blue Sky.

———. 2009. *The Mostly True Adventures of Homer P. Figg*. New York: Blue Sky.

Phillips, S. 2008. *Burn: A Novel*. New York: Little, Brown.

Pilkey, D. 1997. *The Adventures of Captain Underpants: An Epic Novel*. New York: Blue Sky.

Porcellino, J. 2008. *Thoreau at Walden*. New York: Hyperion.

Powell, N. 2008. *Swallow Me Whole*. Marietta, GA: Top Shelf Productions.

Pratchett, T. 2008. *Nation*. New York: HarperCollins.

Prelutsky, J. 1984. *New Kid on the Block*. New York: Greenwillow.

Rathmann, P. 1995. *Officer Buckle and Gloria*. New York: Putnam's.

Rawls, W. 2000. *Where the Red Fern Grows*. St. Paul, MN: EMC/Paradigm.

Reed, G. 2005. *Mary Shelley's Frankenstein: The Graphic Novel*. New York: Puffin Books.

Rex, A. 2008. *Frankenstein Takes the Cake*. Orlando: Harcourt.

Roberts, D., and J. Leslie. 2006. *Pick Me Up: Stuff You Need to Know. . . .* New York: Dorling Kindersley.

Rowling, J. K. 1998. *Harry Potter and the Sorcerer's Stone*. New York: Arthur A. Levine Books.

———. 2000. *Harry Potter and the Goblet of Fire*. New York: Arthur A. Levine Books.

————. 2007. *Harry Potter and the Deathly Hollows*. New York: Arthur A. Levine Books.

Sachar, L. 2008. *Holes*. 10th ann. ed. New York: Farrar, Straus and Giroux.

Saenz, B. A. 2008. *He Forgot to Say Goodbye*. New York: Simon and Schuster Books for Young Readers.

Saldaña, R. Jr. 2007. *The Whole Sky Full of Stars*. New York: Wendy Lamb Books.

Sanderson, B. 2007. *Alcatraz Versus the Evil Librarians*. New York: Scholastic.

San Souci, R. D. 1989. *The Talking Eggs: A Folktale from the American South*. New York: Dial Books for Young Readers.

Schlitz, L. A. 2007. *Good Masters! Sweet Ladies! Voices from a Medieval Village*. Cambridge, MA: Candlewick.

Schmidt, G. D. 2007. *The Wednesday Wars*. New York: Clarion Books.

Schrag, A., ed. 2007. *Stuck in the Middle: Seventeen Comics from an Unpleasant Age*. New York: Viking.

Scieszka, J. 1999. *The True Story of the 3 Little Pigs*. 10th ann. ed. New York: Viking.

————. 2008. *Knucklehead: Tall Tales and Mostly True Stories About Growing Up Scieszka*. New York: Viking Juvenile.

Selzer, A. 2006. *How to Get Suspended and Influence People: A Novel*. New York: Delacorte.

Selznick, B. 2007. *The Invention of Hugo Cabret: A Novel in Words and Pictures*. New York: Scholastic.

Sendak, M. 1991. *Where the Wild Things Are*. 25th ann. ed. New York: HarperCollins.

Shakespeare, W. 2003. *Hamlet*. New York: Penguin.

Shannon, J. 1986. *Too Much T.J.* New York: Delacorte.

Shanower, E. 2006. *Adventures in Oz*. San Diego, CA: IDW Publishing.

Siegel, S. C. 2006. *To Dance: A Ballerina's Graphic Novel*. New York: Richard Jackson Books.

Sís, P. 1996. *Starry Messenger: A Book Depicting the Life of a Famous Scientist, Mathematician, Astronomer, Philosopher, Physicist, Galileo Galilei*. New York: Farrar, Straus, and Giroux.

————. 2007. *The Wall: Growing Up Behind the Iron Curtain*. New York: Farrar, Straus and Giroux.

Sleator, W. 1993. *Oddballs: Stories*. New York: Dutton Children's Books.

Smith, C. L. 2009. *Eternal*. Somerville, MA: Candlewick.

Smith, J. 1994. *Bone: The Complete Cartoon Epic in One Volume*. Ohio: Cartoon Books.

————. 2005. *Bone 1: Out from Boneville*. New York: Graphix.

Smith, L., and R. Fershleiser. 2009. *I Can't Keep My Own Secrets: Six-Word Memoirs by Teens Famous & Obscure*. New York: HarperTeen.

Snicket, L. 2007a. *The Bad Beginning*. A Series of Unfortunate Events Book 1. New York: HarperTrophy.

————. 2007b. *Horseradish: Bitter Truths You Can't Avoid*. New York: HarperCollins.

Sones, S. 1999. *Stop Pretending: What Happened When My Big Sister Went Crazy*. New York: HarperCollins.

————. 2001. *What My Mother Doesn't Know*. New York: Simon and Schuster Books for Young Readers.

Soto, G. 2000. *Chato and the Party Animals*. New York: Putnam.

————. 2006. *A Fire in My Hands: Poems*. Rev. and exp. ed. Orlando: Harcourt.

Spiegelman, A. 1986. *Maus I: A Survivor's Tale: My Father Bleeds History*. New York: Pantheon.

———. 1992. *Maus II: A Survivor's Tale: And Here My Troubles Began*. New York: Pantheon.

Steptoe, J. 1987. *Mufaro's Beautiful Daughters: An African Tale*. New York: Lothrop, Lee and Shepard Books.

Stevens, J.1995. *Tops and Bottoms*. San Diego: Harcourt Brace.

Stevenson, R. L. 2007. *Treasure Island*. Audiobook. Narr. A. Molina. New York: Listening Library.

Stewart, T. L. 2007. *Mysterious Benedict Society*. New York: Little, Brown.

Stoker, B. 2006. *Dracula*. Clayton, DE: Prestwick House.

Swain, R. F. 2008. *Underwear: What We Wear Under There*. New York: Holiday House.

Tamaki, M. 2008. *Skim*. Toronto, ON, Canada: Groundwood Books.

Tan, S. 2007. *The Arrival*. New York : Arthur A. Levine Books.

Thurber, J. 1990. *The Wonderful O*. New York: D. I. Fine.

Tomasi, P. J. 2005. *Light Brigade*. New York: DC Comics.

Van Allsburg, C. 1981. *Jumanji*. Boston: Houghton Mifflin.

Van Draanen, W. 1998. *Sammy Keyes and the Hotel Thief*. New York: Knopf.

Vaught, S. 2008. *Exposed*. New York: Bloomsbury.

Voigt, C. 2005. *Izzy, Willy-Nilly*. New York: Simon Pulse.

Wallace, R. 1996. *Wrestling Sturbridge*. New York: Alfred A. Knopf.

———. 2007. *One Good Punch*. New York: Alfred A. Knopf.

Warren, F. 2005. *PostSecret: Extraordinary Confessions from Ordinary Lives*. New York: ReganBooks.

Wasserman, R. 2008. *Skinned*. New York: Simon Pulse.

Waters, D. 2008. *Generation Dead*. New York: Hyperion.

Weatherford, C. B. 2007. *Birmingham, 1963*. Honesdale, PA: Wordsong.

Weaver, W. 1993. *Striking Out*. New York: HarperCollins.

———. 1995. *Farm Team*. New York: HarperCollins.

———. 1998. *Hard Ball: A Billy Baggs Novel*. New York: HarperCollins.

Westerfeld, S. 2007. *Extras*. New York: Simon Pulse.

White, E. B. 2006. *Charlotte's Web*. New York: HarperCollins.

Wiesner, D. 2001. *The Three Pigs*. New York: Clarion Books.

———. 2006. *Flotsam*. New York: Clarion Books.

Williams, J. 2004. *Escaping Tornado Season: A Story in Poems*. New York: HarperTempest.

Winick, J. 2000. *Pedro and Me: Friendship, Loss, and What I Learned*. New York: Henry Holt.

Wolff, V. E. 1993. *Make Lemonade*. New York: Henry Holt.

———. 2001. *True Believer*. New York: Atheneum Books for Young Readers.

———. 2009. *This Full House*. New York: Bowen.

Wood, A. 1994. *Quick as a Cricket*. New York: Scholastic.

Wood, D. 2008. *Into the Volcano: A Graphic Novel*. New York: Blue Sky.

Woodson, J. 1998. *If You Come Softly*. New York: G. P. Putnam's Sons.

Yang, G. L. 2006. *American Born Chinese*. New York: First Second.

Yee, L. 2003. *Millicent Min, Girl Genius*. New York: Arthur A. Levine Books.

———. 2005. *Stanford Wong Flunks Big-Time*. New York: Arthur A. Levine Books.

———. 2007. *So Totally Emily Ebers*. New York: Arthur A. Levine Books.

———. 2009. *Absolutely Maybe*. New York: Arthur A. Levine Books.

Yorinks, A. 1986. *Hey, Al*. New York: Farrar, Straus and Giroux.

Young, E. 1989. *Lon Po Po: A Red-Riding Hood Story from China*. New York: Philomel Books.

———. 2007. *Seven Blind Mice*. Audiobook. Narr. B. D. Wong. Norwalk, CT: Weston Woods Studios.

Zevin, G. 2007. *Memoirs of a Teenage Amnesiac*. New York: Farrar, Straus and Giroux.

Zimmer, T. V. 2008. *42 Miles*. New York: Clarion Books.

Zindel, P. 2005. *The Pigman*. New York: HarperTrophy.

Zusak, M. 2007. *The Book Thief*. New York: Knopf.

Professional Text Bibliography

Here are the professional books mentioned throughout the text. Online resources are invaluable to me when I search for books or seek bibliographic information. Amazon (www.amazon.com/) is one option for finding information. Titlewave (www.titlewave.com/) is another, and anyone can open a free Titlewave account, which gives you access to not only bibliographic information but full-text reviews of books as well.

Applebee, A. 1991. *A Study of High School Literature Anthologies*. Report Series 1.5. Albany, NY: National Research Center on English Learning and Achievement. cela.albany.edu/reports/applebee/applebeestudy/index.html.

Atwell, N. 1998. *In the Middle: New Understandings About Writing, Reading, and Learning*. 2d ed. Portsmouth, NH: Boynton/Cook.

Beers, G. K., and T. Lesesne. 2001. *Books for You: An Annotated Booklist for Senior High*. Urbana, IL: National Council of Teachers of English.

Beers, K., R. E. Probst, and L. Rief, eds. 2007. *Adolescent Literacy: Turning Promise into Practice*. Portsmouth, NH: Heinemann.

Bird, S. 2005. A Content Analysis of the Most Commonly Adopted High School Literature Anthologies. Unpublished doctoral dissertation. Houston, TX: University of Houston.

Brown, J. 2003. *Your Reading: An Annotated Booklist for Middle School and Junior High*. Urbana, IL: National Council of Teachers of English.

Clark, R. C. 2009. "Listening to Teens Talk Back: Teen Responses to Booktalking Styles." *Voice of Youth Advocates* 31 (6): 501–4.

Daniels, H. 2002. *Literature Circles: Voice and Choice in Book Clubs and Reading Groups*. 2d ed. Portland, ME: Stenhouse.

Daniels, H., and N. Steineke. 2004. *Mini-lessons for Literature Circles*. Portsmouth, NH: Heinemann.

Fontichiaro, K. 2008. *Podcasting at School*. Westport, CT: Libraries Unlimited.

Fox, M. 2008. *Reading Magic: Why Reading Aloud to Our Children Will Change Their Lives Forever*. Upd. and rev. ed. Orlando: Harcourt.

Friedman, T. L. 2007. *The World Is Flat: A Brief History of the Twenty-First Century*. New York: Farrar, Straus and Giroux.

Gibson, K. S. 2004. A Survey of Elementary Student's Attitudes Toward Reading Motivation Activities. Unpublished doctoral dissertation. Houston, TX: University of Houston.

Giles, V. M. 2005. Secondary School Students' (Grades 7–12) Attitudes Toward Reading Motivational Activities. Unpublished doctoral dissertation. Houston, TX: University of Houston.

Herald, D. T. 2006. *Genreflecting: A Guide to Popular Reading Interests.* Westport, CT: Libraries Unlimited.

Herz, S. K., and D. R. Gallo. 2005. *From Hinton to Hamlet: Building Bridges Between Young Adult Literature and the Classics.* Westport, CT: Greenwood.

Kaywell, J. F. 2008. *Adolescent Literature as a Complement to the Classics: Addressing Critical Issues in Today's Classrooms.* Norwood, MA: Christopher-Gordon.

Krashen, S. 2008. The Case for Libraries and Librarians. Invited Paper, Submitted to the Obama-Biden Education Policy Working Group, December, 2008.

Larson, J. 2004. *Bringing Mysteries Alive for Children and Young Adults.* Worthington, OH: Linworth.

Lesesne, T. S. 2003. *Making the Match: The Right Book for the Right Reader at the Right Time, Grades 4–12.* Portland, ME: Stenhouse.

———. 2006. *Naked Reading: Uncovering What Tweens Need to Become Lifelong Readers.* Portland, ME: Stenhouse.

Livaudais, M. 1986. A Survey of Secondary Students' Attitudes Toward Reading Motivational Activities. Unpublished doctoral dissertation. Houston, TX: University of Houston.

Marshall, J. C. 2002. *Are They Really Reading? Expanding SSR in the Middle Grades.* Portland, ME: Stenhouse.

Martinez, A. 1989. A Meta-Analysis of Reading Aloud. Unpublished paper. Houston, TX: Phi Delta Kappa Seminar, University of Houston.

Pilgreen, J. L. 2000. *The SSR Handbook: How to Organize and Manage a Sustained Silent Reading Program.* Portsmouth, NH: Heinemann.

Pink, D. H. 2005. *A Whole New Mind: Why Right-Brainers Will Rule the Future.* New York: Riverhead Books.

Potter, M. 2009. "Top Shelf Fiction." *Voice of Youth Advocates* (February 2009): 490.

Sherrill, A., and G. R. Carlsen. 1988. *Voices of Readers: How We Come to Love Books.* Urbana, IL: NCTE.

Trelease, J. 2006. *The Read-Aloud Handbook.* 6th ed. New York: Penguin Books.

Possible Themes for Reading Ladders

The possibilities are truly endless. Reading ladders can be constructed on any subject or theme. They can be related to many curricular areas as well. Here are topics with some suggestions about where to begin and how to proceed with construction.

Betrayal

Betrayal is a classic theme that's broad enough so that many titles could become part of the ladder we construct. How about beginning with a traditional story complete with archetypes, such as *Cinderella*? Cinderella's father betrays his own child in the Grimm version of the tale, telling the prince that he does not have a third daughter. This base of the ladder could offer us the chance to explore fairy tale variants including contemporary ones that occasionally are satires or parodies of the traditional tales. *Bubba the Cowboy Prince* (Ketteman 1997) is a Texas Cinderella story with a fairy god-cow. Or perhaps we could explore other cultures with Korean, Cajun, Irish, African, and other versions of the story.

Drama

My next example is a genre-based reading ladder focusing on dramatic works. I include it here because I think one of the stumbling blocks with the study of Shakespeare in upper grades has to do with students' unfamiliarity with how to approach this type of text on paper. Perhaps we can begin building some background knowledge and experience (scaffolding) by sharing plays with students earlier. Incorporating some readers theatre (RT) along the way might also prove beneficial. So, we could begin with some simple scripts. Aaron Shepard (www.aaronshep.com/) maintains an incredible website with some free scripts that we could use as the base for this reading ladder. Use this site as a resource for ideas for teaching students to prepare RT scripts, and your classes can actually compose the scripts to use as they climb this ladder. Some other titles to search for include Don Gallo's *Center Stage* (1990), a collection of one-act plays written by YA authors, *Acting Out* (2008), six one-act plays written by Newbery-winning authors including Avi and Katherine Paterson, and *Acting Natural*, by Peg Kehret (1991), which contains monologues, dialogues, and short plays for performance. Once students are adept, they could adapt some Shakespearean scenes for RT performance as well.

Exploration of the Inner Person

Works that focus on the inner part of the character or nonfiction works that are introspective can be tough choices unless we build the foundation for accessing these stories. Often the first encounter with these texts occurs in high school when students first meet Emerson and Thoreau. If we introduce students in middle school to some of this work, then their high school encounters will be, hopefully, more successful. One of my favorite books for a step (not necessarily the base) of this reading ladder is *Thoreau at Walden*, by John Porcellino (2008). Porcellino utilizes his graphic arts background in this simple adaptation that uses Thoreau's own words along with spare illustrations. We might also include some autobiographical works. From Gary Paulsen's *Schernoff Discoveries* (1997) to Jack Gantos' *Hole in My Life* (2002), the YA field offers an array of books from the humorous to the intense. Note that I do not have a particular base in mind for this ladder. Once we are confident in our ability to construct ladders, we might read a book that we know will fall into a theme or topic. It might not be the base or the pinnacle. It may be the sole book we have for the moment. However, if we keep a running list of themes and topics to explore, we can jot down the titles as we discover them, knowing that, down the road, we will have what we need to construct the entire ladder. This could also be an instance where we provide our students with one of the steps and allow them to construct a ladder around that one title.

Fantasy

Fantasy is an often overlooked genre in middle and high school. The novels of J. K. Rowling have done much to bring fantasy back to the forefront. However, there is much more to the genre than Harry Potter. Fantasy is important in the development of readers because it explores ancient themes. Many of the characters are archetypal. Settings are essential to the story and often play as important a role as the characters do. Exploring fantasy might be one topic that could stretch across all the secondary grades. What to include? *The Hunger Games*, by Suzanne Collins (2008), *The Adoration of Jenna Fox*, by Mary Pearson (2008), and *Little Brother*, by Cory Doctorow (2008), are three dystopic novels that can lead eventually to the more classic novels *1984* (Orwell 2007) and *Brave New World* (Huxley 1989). Vampire novels, a hot trend of the past decade, would work here as well. Imagine culminating the vampire sequence with *Dracula* (Stoker 2006). Story collections might also be something to consider for this ladder.

Graphic Novels

Once graphic novels were both few in number and limited in their classroom utility because of mature content. Now this format has entered into the mainstream with graphic adaptations of Nancy Drew and the Baby-Sitters Club. Adaptations of other series and titles are also part of a recent trend. *Artemis Fowl* is now in graphic novel adaptation (Colfer and Donkin 2007), as are the Pendragon books, by D. J. MacHale, and the Redwall series, by Brian Jacques. Graphic novels are available for very young readers as well; see, for example, *BabyMouse*, by Jennifer and Matthew Holm (2005). I like to begin with the simple BabyMouse series because, visually, it picks up on some important aspects of the entire field. For those not familiar with the series, BabyMouse is a plucky young mouse who loves most everything in life. However, her inner life is often more rewarding than the reality of her situation. Illustrations are in black and white with touches of pink. So, BabyMouse can assist us in discussing the use of color to establish mood or to highlight something important in a story (symbolism). It can also lead us into a discussion of character development. Because the text and illustrations are deceptively simple, all students should be able to access them readily. From this bottom rung, we can proceed with more and more complex graphic novels, ending with *Maus I* and *Maus II*, by Art Spiegelman (1986 and 1992). For more titles, check out YALSA's "Great Graphic Novels for Teens" list at www.ala.org/yalsa.

Historical Fiction

Content area reading ladders are important. They provide us one way to collaborate with our colleagues in the other disciplines, for one thing. Also, I think given our background, we can better select developmentally appropriate books to use in social studies classes. Reading ladders here will depend on the scope of the course at a particular grade level. So, instead of offering titles here, let me instead offer an important resource. Each year, the National Council for the Social Studies and the Children's Book Council collaborate to produce a list of books suitable for social studies classrooms. Books on the "Notable Social Studies Trade Books for Young People" list, therefore, have the endorsement of both those who know accuracy on historical works and those who know the features of the best books for children and teens. The list encompasses books for K–12. Information on this list is available at www.socialstudies.org/notable. Another list to consider is the list of Orbis Pictus winners from the National Council of Teachers of English (www.ncte.org/awards/orbispictus), which recognizes excellence in nonfiction for children.

Love

Ah, love. Yes, this might be a females-only ladder. However, it does not have to be that limiting. One of the ladders I find helpful is the one with Shakespeare's *Romeo and Juliet* on the top rung. Below are books such as *Romiette and Julio*, by Sharon Draper (2001), and *If You Come Softly*, by Jacqueline Woodson (1998). Both of these are contemporary reworkings of Shakespeare's classic. Another direction to head here includes variations on the theme such as forbidden love (Meyer's *Twilight* [2005]), love unrequited (Shannon's *Too Much T.J.* [1986]), love gone bad (Gregerson's *Bad Girls Club* [2007]), and obsessive love (Cormier's *Tenderness* [1997]). Anti-Valentine's themes (Anderson's *Prom* [2005]) can be wildly popular, too. Remember that love can also be love for a treasured pet (*Shiloh* [Naylor 1991] anyone?) or love for family (Giff's *Pictures of Hollis Wood* [2002]) or even love of country (Crane's *The Red Badge of Courage* [2005]).

Poetry

There is a huge gap between poetry offered to children and that offered to young adults. Many students are asked to move from Shel Silverstein, Jack Prelutsky, and J. Patrick Lewis to Robert Frost and Emily Dickinson. A huge chasm exists between these two groups of poets, a chasm that could cause students to slip and fall headlong into a dark hole, never to emerge. Why not construct a ladder that bridges this chasm? For that to occur, we have to move students slowly, sometimes horizontally a few steps before moving vertically can be safe. One factor to keep in mind while constructing a poetry ladder is that the topic or subject of the poem needs to be within the realm of experience of the reader. "Stopping by Woods on a Snowy Evening" was most definitely not something most of my middle school students could connect with immediately. To begin with, most of them had never seen snow, let alone an open field filling up with snow on a moonlit evening. Likewise, the poems of Emily Dickinson did not have much meaning to my students, whose own life experiences are quite different from hers. So, locating poems about the life experiences of our students is crucial. Living authors are more likely to offer these reading experiences. Often, our students think one of the requirements for becoming a poet is to be dead already. Showing them that living, breathing folks write poetry that might interest them is one place to begin the crafting of this ladder, then. The National Council of Teachers of English awards a living poet its Excellence in Poetry for Children for his or her body of work. Perhaps we can begin with the work of one of the contemporary poets listed here: www.ncte.org/awards/poetry.

Science (Fiction and Nonfiction)

Just as books with historical content must meet different requirements, so it is with science. The Children's Book Council in conjunction with the National Science Teachers Association compiles an annual list of the best books for use in the K–12 science curriculum. Information about the list can be accessed at http://www.nsta.org/publications/ostb/. The Orbis Pictus Award for excellence in nonfiction books for children is another helpful resource (www.ncte.org/awards/orbispictus).

Don't forget that science fiction can be used effectively within the science curriculum as well.

Short Stories

Often, a study of short stories was the first "unit" I did in English class with my middle school students. I quickly discovered that the short story suffered in much the same way that poetry did in my literature anthologies and textbooks: the stories contained in these collections did not speak to contemporary teens as they did to previous generations. Don Gallo, retired professor and noted expert in the field of YA literature, began publishing story collections in the 1980s. Each collection is themed and contains stories written by some of the most talented authors of YA literature. *Sixteen*, *Connections*, *Visions*, *Within Reach*, *Short Circuit*, *Destination Unexpected*, *What Are You Afraid Of?* and *Owning It* are among the titles of his collections, which cover topics as diverse as literal and figurative journeys, phobias, and disabilities. Margo Lanagan's Printz Honor book, *Black Juice* (2005), is a story collection especially suited for older teens. Neil Gaiman offers an homage to the short stories of Ray Bradbury (can you see this reading ladder taking a turn now?) in *M Is for Magic* (2007). *Tomorrowland*, edited by Michael Cart (1999), is a collection focused on a new millennium and what it might hold. James Howe and Lois Lowry also have anthologies of short stories. Chris Crutcher's *Athletic Shorts* (1991) uses characters from his novels, situating them in stories set sometimes before and sometimes after the events of the longer works. There is another leaping point for a potential reading ladder.

Sports

Since I offered love as a theme, I thought I might balance things out a bit by suggesting sports as a potential theme or topic for a reading ladder. While sports is not exclusively male in its focus, it does tend to lean in that direction a bit. Of course, we do not want to pigeonhole something as a sports book. Most novels that feature athletes and sports deal with other themes and issues such as power, competition, accomplishment, and dedication. Sports might be the way in for some reluctant readers, however, so let's explore some of what we can build into this reading ladder. Works by Will Weaver, especially *Farm Team* (1995), *Striking Out* (1993), and *Hard Ball* (1998), belong here, as do some of the works of Carl Deuker, including *Runner* (2007b), *Gym Candy* (2007a), and *Heart of a Champion* (1993). *Wrestling Sturbridge* (1996) and *One Good Punch* (2007), by Rich Wallace, would be logical choices for the ladder, along with works by Crutcher, some by Lynch, and Catherine Murdock's *Dairy Queen* (2006) and *The Off Season* (2007). Chris Crowe's *More than a Game: Sports Literature for Young Adults* (2004) would be an excellent resource to have on hand during the building of sports ladders.

Final Note

The possibilities are, indeed, limitless. Any subject, topic, theme, concept, or idea can morph into the beginning of a reading ladder. And the more we read, the more possibilities are open to us.

Index